D0007532

TWAYNE'S WORLD AUTHOR SERIES

A Survey of the World's Literature

Sylvia E. Bowman, Indiana University

GENERAL EDITOR

AUSTRIA

Ulrich Weisstein, Indiana University

EDITOR

Oswald von Wolkenstein

(TWAS 236)

TWAYNE'S WORLD AUTHORS SERIES (TWAS)

The purpose of TWAS is to survey the major writers —novelists, dramatists, historians, poets, philosophers, and critics—of the nations of the world. Among the national literatures covered are those of Australia, Canada, China, Eastern Europe, France, Germany, Greece, India, Italy, Japan, Latin America, the Netherlands, New Zealand, Poland, Russia, Scandinavia, Spain, and the African nations, as well as Hebrew, Yiddish, and Latin Classical literatures. This survey is complemented by Twayne's United States Authors Series and English Authors Series.

The intent of each volume in these series is to present a critical-analytical study of the works of the writer; to include biographical and historical material that may be necessary for understanding, appreciation, and critical appraisal of the writer and to present all material in clear, concise English—but not to vitiate the scholarly content of the work by doing so.

Oswald von Wolkenstein

By GEORGE F. JONES

University of Maryland

Twayne Publishers, Inc. :: New York

Library of Congress Catalog Card Number: 72-39776

MANUFACTURED IN THE UNITED STATES OF AMERICA

Preface

Oswald von Wolkenstein was the first medieval German poet whose works survive in an entirely reliable form; for he left two handsome manuscripts, both of which have been well preserved and are completely legible. The first of these, MS A, in the National Library in Vienna, was completed in 1425; the second, MS B, in the University Library in Innsbruck, was written in 1432, with a few later additions. Except for the spelling and the order of the songs, these texts are remarkably close to each other; and there are indications that the author supervised their compilation. A paper manuscript, MS C, in the Ferdinandeum Museum in Innsbruck, was copied from MS B and therefore contributes nothing new, except that the scribe occasionally corrected obvious scribal errors on the part of his predecessor.

Because Oswald was a man of political and social importance, we have copious documentary evidence about his life, much of it gathered and collated by Count Arthur von Wolkenstein-Rodenegg, who, although a direct descendant, wrote a completely objective Oswald biography in 1930.[1] Since then a modicum of new material has come to light and some old documents have been reinterpreted, but this scarcely alters the overall picture Wolkenstein-Rodenegg has outlined. Regrettably, his biography treats only the man and the politician Oswald, and neglects the poet. Additional data about Oswald's life have been supplied in the dissertations of Norbert Mayr and Ulrich Müller.

Wolkenstein's two handsome parchment manuscripts remained in his family's possession, and only a few of his songs were disseminated in popular songbooks like that of Clara Hätzler.[2] Consequently, his songs were soon forgotten and remained lost for centuries before being brought to light in 1847 in an edition by a Dominican priest named Beda Weber. Unfortunately, Weber also wrote a semischolarly, semifantastic biography—one might almost say a historical novel—entitled *Oswald von Wolkenstein and Frederick with the Empty Purse,*[3] which deals largely with the struggles between Oswald and his Tyrolian overlord. Where Oswald's songs failed to furnish details, Weber supplied them from his own vivid imagination and thus created a myth that pervaded Wolkenstein scholarship until only a decade or so ago, when it was finally questioned by Norbert Mayr and again by Ulrich Müller. Weber documented many of his assertions by citing certain *Reisenotata,* or travel notes, which have since disappeared. It has now been ascertained that, unless these notes were merely figments of Weber's imagination, they must have been made by one of Oswald's descendants in trying to establish some chronology for the facts related in his travel songs. Because of the inaccuracies introduced by Weber but accepted as facts by his successors, it is best for the beginning student to read the latest criticism first and only then risk exposure to the older and unfounded views.

Unable to cope with Oswald's songs, scholars initially busied themselves mainly with the man rather than with the poet. Most of the events of Oswald's life can be ascertained only approximately, often just as falling between two documented dates. Whereas the exact dates of his birth and death are unknown, there is evidence that he was not yet born near the end of 1376 and that he was already born by early 1378. This indicates that his birth probably occurred in 1377, or possibly in the last weeks of 1376 or the first weeks of 1378. Should a document confirming one of the latter two dates be found, then many dates in this study would have to be adjusted accordingly. This would, however, in no way alter our understanding or appreciation of Oswald's songs. We know that Oswald was still alive on June 18, 1445, and that he was already dead on August 2 of that year; but we do not know on precisely which day he died. The place of his birth is now generally assumed to have been Schöneck Castle near Bruneck (now Brunico), where his father resided in 1377.

The present study is based on MS B, using both photostats of the original and the edition of the late Karl Kurt Klein. The quoted passages differ from Klein's edition mostly in matters of punctuation. Since the manuscript has no punctuation except for the slash (/), which served as a signal for the singer, I have taken the liberty of punctuating and capitalizing as I deem most useful for the English-speaking reader. It will be noted that, from an Anglo-Saxon viewpoint, Oswald's thoughts can best be written in sentences of two or four verses, rather than in the long compound ones preferred by the German editors.

The only other freedom I have taken with the text is to resolve the dieresis (¨), which the scribe of MS B used for many purposes, for example, to indicate umlaut *(göttlich, sünde)*, diphthong *(güt, hüt)*, umlauted diphthong *(süssen, füssen)*, and vowel length *(wän, här)*, or for no apparent reason whatever *(paü, swër, wër)*. The same word may appear indiscriminately with or without the dieresis: *wän* (20/38) = *wan* (26/121). To avoid any possible confusion, I have retained the dieresis only to indicate umlaut *(zärtlich, göttlich, über)* and have resolved the diphthong *ü* as *uo* and *üe (guot, süess)* in accordance with standard Middle High German spelling. The spelling *ue* in MS A proves that these letters were intended as diphthongs, as they still are in Bavarian. Where the dieresis signified nothing but the scribe's whim, it has been ignored. In a few cases, in order to make rhymes more visual, I have altered the archaic and exceptional spelling *in* to *ein*, when it rhymes with a word spelled that way. I have also occásionally placed an acúte áccent on syllables that would not bear the stress if spoken instead of sung.

As we shall see, Oswald was immensely proud of his birth and family and often mentioned himself in his songs, always as Wolkenstein. Although he never referred to himself as Oswald, we shall do so most of the time, if for no other reason than that it is shorter and unambiguous, and that we Americans now live in a first-name society. The names of important personages appear as they are known in the English-speaking world: Friedrich appears as Frederick and Sigmund as Sigismund. The medieval poets gave no titles to their songs; and therefore we use the first verse as a title, even if it is neither descriptive nor significant. A few of the more frequently mentioned songs have been given simpler and easier-to-remember designations such as the Augsburg song, the Hussite song, and the Hauenstein song. To simplify typesetting, cross-references to songs quoted or mentioned in the text omit the page number and give only the title or designation of the song, which can be quickly located by consulting the appended song-index.

The greatest stumbling block on the slow road to a better understanding of Oswald's songs has been the gulf separating the many literary historians and the few musicologists who have dealt with him. The first, and until recently the only, major study devoted to his music—Herbert Löwenstein's dissertation of 1932—had a literary orientation; and the latest edition of Oswald's songs (that by Karl Kurt Klein) is written primarily for the literary critic, although some of the melodies are appended. The gulf between literary historians and musicologists is gradually closing through the efforts of scholars like Christoph Petzsch, Walter Röll, Walter Salmen, Franz Viktor Spechtler, and Josef Wendler, who are competent in music as well as literature. Wendler's dissertation treats Oswald from a musicological perspective and is all but unintelligible to the non-musicologist. Unfortunately, because of my incompetence in musical matters, the present volume must restrict itself to Oswald the poet, rather than extending to Oswald the composer; but I hope that musicologists will be tolerant of the resulting biases and errors. I further hope that this book may inspire some trained musicologist, perhaps even one unfamiliar with German literature, to use it as a basis for a study that will do justice to Oswald's melodies as well as to his lyrics. These melodies were well recorded and preserved in both MS A and MS B; and they are the earliest German works to be written down, in part, in the mensural notation that had already been well developed in France, Burgundy, and Italy.

It would be unfeasible in a work of this type to acknowledge each and every bit of help I have received from previous Oswald critics, especially so because many ideas have developed gradually while being passed down from one scholar to the other. Therefore, I wish to recognize my indebtedness to all those who have cast light on the subject. Of recent contributors, the most helpful have been Frank Banta, Gerhard Eis, William T. H. Jackson, Karl Kurt Klein, Otto Mann, Fritz Martini, Friedrich Maurer, Norbert Mayr, Ulrich Müller, Lambertus Okken, Christoph Petzsch, Walter Salmen, Franz Viktor Spechtler, and Eugen Thurnher.

To save space and avoid an air of dull pedantry, I have not documented my statements of fact, most of which have been corroborated in the works named in the notes and bibliography. All conjectures and subjective evaluations are my own, even if sometimes first suggested by my predecessors. If the word "probably" seems overworked (together with circumlocutions such as "seems to have," "could have been," etc.), it is because caution often dissuaded me from saying "surely" or "certainly." The footnotes are limited to explanations and hints for further reading. When reference is made to "Herbert Löwenstein's dissertation" or to "the edition of Karl Kurt Klein," these can be quickly found in the bibliography. It is hoped that the nonspecialist will pardon the apparent quibbling about dates, which the author has included to justify his conjectures about the chronology of many of the songs. No use has been made of the, perhaps premature, chronology offered by W. Marold in 1926, which has been uncritically accepted by many recent scholars. Uncommon literary terms and Middle High German expressions used in this study are explained the first time they appear; if repeated, they are listed in the index, which indicates the page on which they are explained.

At this time I wish to thank my seminarists at both the University of Maryland and the University of Munich for the ideas they have stimulated. To the American Philosophical Society is owed the trip to Europe which enabled me to visit the Wolkenstein Archives of the Germanic Museum in Nuremberg, the library of the University of Innsbruck, where MS B and much other Oswaldiana are stored, and also Oswald's various castles in South Tyrol. The Research Grant Board of the University of Maryland deserves thanks for financing the typing of this monograph.

University of Maryland GEORGE FENWICK JONES

Contents

Chronology

1377 Oswald born at Schöneck Castle.
1378 Great Schism begins.
1386 Battle of Sempach in Switzerland, death blow to independent knighthood.
1387 Oswald sets out on his travels.
1389 Sabina born.
1396 Battle of Nikopolis.
1397 Agreement with the Jägers giving Oswald's father one-third of Hauenstein.
1399 Death of Oswald's father.
1400 King Wenzel deposed on August 20, Ruprecht of the Palatinate elected Roman King.
1402 Oswald accompanies Ruprecht to Italy.
1406 Elephant League founded on August 23.
1407 Falcon League founded on March 28. Wolkenstein properties divided among three sons on April 22, Oswald receives Hauenstein. Oswald meets Sabina?
1408 Oswald endows chapel dedicated to St. Oswald at Brixen.
1409 Oswald nominated Captain of the Cloister at Brixen. Sabina's husband dies. Oswald departs for the Holy Land.
1410 Ruprecht dies; Sigismund elected on September 20.
1414 Beginning of Council of Constance.
1415 Oswald arrives in Constance on February 4, enters Sigismund's service on February 16. Sent on mission to Spain on March 20, participates in campaign of King John of Portugal against the Moors; present at capture of Ceuta on August 21.

Sigismund arrives in Perpignan on September 18, continues to Narbonne on November 5. Alienates Iberian kingdoms from Pope Benedict.

1416 End of Schism celebrated in Avignon early in January. Sigismund received in Paris on March 1. He continues to London on April 6. Oswald returns to Constance.

1417 Oswald with Sigismund in Constance on January 27. Duke Frederick outlawed, Sigismund promises help to Tyrolian nobles. Oswald marries Margaret of Schwangau.

1418 Siege of Greifenstein in March. Sigismund and Frederick reconciled on March 10.

1419 Oswald in Hungary on March 1.

1420 Oswald participates in Hussite crusade?

1421 Oswald captured by Jägers early in the fall, put in custody of Duke Frederick on December 17.

1422 Oswald liberated on March 18, returns to captivity on August 21 and so remains until December 23, 1423.

1423 Frederick again outlawed, imperial army raised. Nobles' League reconciled with Frederick, and their rights confirmed. Oswald freed in general amnesty.

1424 Journey to Pressburg in the fall.

1425 Frederick and Sigismund reconciled on February 27 because of troubles with Hussites. Sabina dies in midsummer. Oswald visits Pressburg (Bratislava). MS A written, continued until 1427, with additions to 1436.

1426 Michael of Wolkenstein reconciled with Frederick, Oswald continues to fight. Oswald at Hauenstein Castle, writes letter on September 9 to Rhinegrave Ludwig about pilgrimage to Palestine.

1427 Oswald misses court at Bozen on March 16, apprehended by Frederick. Reconciled with Frederick on May 1, end of struggle for Hauenstein.

1428 Oswald journeys to Cologne, becomes magistrate of *Femegericht.*

1430 Oswald attends Diet of Nuremberg, visits Augsburg, Constance, and Ulm in imperial service.

1431 Oswald participates in the Hussite crusade? Imperial forces defeated at Taus on August 14. Joan of Arc burned, François Villon born.

1432 Oswald in Sigismund's chancelry in Piacenza and then in Parma. Sigismund's envoys attacked at Ronciglione. Oswald accompanies Dr. Stock to Council of Basel on May 30. MS B completed, additional songs until 1438.

Chronology

1433 Sigismund crowned emperor at Rome on May 31.
1439 Frederick dies on June 24.
1445 Oswald dies in midsummer.
1450 Gutenberg perfects movable type.
1453 Fall of Constantinople to the Turks. End of Hundred Years' War.

CHAPTER 1

Early Life

I *The Historical Background*

A STUDY of Oswald von Wolkenstein's songs would benefit from a knowledge of the classical Middle High German poets Hartmann von Aue, Wolfram von Eschenbach, Gottfried von Strassburg, and Walther von der Vogelweide. The last of these, Walther, has been the subject of an earlier volume in this series,[1] which attempts to give an idea of the cultural environment in which he lived.

Although Walther von der Vogelweide and Oswald von Wolkenstein both belonged to the Middle Ages, the latter was, in many respects, closer to us moderns. Walther had lived in the High Middle Ages, which, in Germany, coincided with the reign of the Hohenstaufen emperors (1152–1254). This was, or at least started out to be, a period of idealism and optimism. Oswald, however, lived in the Late Middle Ages, which was a period of realism, pessimism, and disillusionment. During the reign of Frederick Barbarossa (1152–90), German scholars like Otto of Freising could arouse and maintain enthusiasm for the Roman Empire, an earthly kingdom divinely ordained to unite all Christians under the spiritual rule of the Pope and the secular rule of the German emperor. Actually, the empire was rarely more than a loosely knit league of German territories, with the addition of some French language areas in the west, some Italian areas in the south, and a Czech enclave in the east. But this was a Platonic age, in which many people—in fact most thinking people—accepted the ideal as real; and many Germans considered the Roman Empire, which was just then acquiring its epithet "Holy," to be an actual and divinely decreed entity for which one could fight and die.

Even before Walther's death, however, it had become evident that the Holy Roman Empire was no more than a dream. As

Walther complained in his political songs, Pope Innocent III sowed discord and incited the selfish territorial rulers against their emperor, whoever he might be, in order to keep Germany in a state of anarchy and thus maintain the political power of the papacy in Italy. During the Great Interregnum from 1254 to 1273 there was no emperor at all, and Germany was ravaged by constant civil war. When the electors finally agreed on an emperor, they purposely chose an inconspicuous princeling, Rudolf of Hapsburg, who held modest lands in Switzerland, Swabia, and Alsace, because they felt sure they could dominate him and thus retain their own freedom of action. In this they were mistaken, for Rudolf exploited his new position to aggrandize his own holdings, for example, by acquiring Austria (a geographical term then referring to lower Austria or the region around Vienna) and Styria, until he became strong enough to master the situation. But, like other emperors before and after him, he too used his sacred office to increase the power of his own household rather than that of the imperial office.

The Christian church fared little better than the empire, for, as Walther once remarked, when the pope sinned, all Christendom sinned with him. Most incumbents of the papal chair did not live up to the standards expected of them; many were merely pawns in the hands of the secular rulers. In 1305, seventy-two years before Oswald's birth, Pope Clement V sought refuge in Avignon, where he and subsequent popes were detained as puppets of the French kings. Then, in 1378, when Oswald was one year old, the Great Schism began, with Urban VI elected pope in Rome while Clement VII still claimed the office in Avignon.

In the moral breakdown of the Late Middle Ages, the old ideals seem to have been forgotten by all but a few dreamers, such as the anonymous author of the *Reformatio Sigismundi,* a treatise advising Emperor Sigismund how to reform the Empire. Oswald was probably typical of his age in his total lack of ideals, in either the philosophic or moral sense of the word. He was basically interested in things rather than ideas, and he championed no cause unless it directly benefited him. He served his emperor for three hundred Hungarian guilders a year, and he fought against heresy when heretics interfered with his plans. But the least we can say for him is that he was no hypocrite, as many people had been in Walther's idealistic age.

There were numerous causes for disillusion and despair in the Late Middle Ages. The Church had promised success in the crusades; yet these invariably failed because of the petty bickerings and jealousies of the Christian leaders. Heresies were rampant; and cruel repression served only to spread them further. It was a period of social upheaval, with rapid changes in both social and economic structure. The old tripartite division of society into clerics, knights, and peasants had been upset by the emergence of the bourgeoisie, whose money and power could no longer be ignored. Capitalism was well entrenched, usury brought greater profits than could be gained through plunder and pillage, and many a spendthrift knight saw his castle taken when he could no longer pay his mortgage. Seven years before Oswald's birth, the proud burghers of the Hanseatic League had compelled the great monarch Waldemar of Denmark to ratify the Peace of Stralsund, which assured the league of economic privileges in Denmark and even gave them the right to veto succession to the Danish throne.

Everywhere the old order was giving way to the new. A short way to the west of Oswald's home, the sturdy Swiss peasants of the Forest Cantons had inflicted ignominious defeats on the flower of Austrian knighthood at Morgarten in 1315 and at Sempach in 1385. The patricians of the South German cities were having their troubles too, as the artisan guilds successfully competed for a voice in municipal affairs. With the breakdown of law and order, the cities had to defend themselves against the robber barons, whose only response to the new money economy was to rob the merchants or seize the lands of their neighbors.

To add to this religious, political, and economic disillusionment, Europe was visited by the Black Death, a bubonic plague that struck Germany for the first time in 1348 and then returned again and again. The prevalence of death, particularly unshriven death, led to mass hysteria; and hordes of penitents roamed through the country, often flagellating themselves, in the hope of winning divine mercy. Literature, art, and public spectacles emphasized the ephemeral nature of life and the omnipresence of death. As in Dürer's famous engraving of a century later, Death was forever following the knight. Except for a new inwardness developing among the mystics and certain pious lay and clerical groups, religion was mostly external and consisted largely of carefully calculated worship and good works, salvation being a commodity that could be measured in monetary terms.

Oswald's songs excellently reflect most of the trends of his age. His life was relatively long and exceptionally active and varied; and his songs convey subjective impressions of everything he experienced. We must remember, however, that he was not a historian. If we are looking for objective facts, we should consult the chronicles of the time, many of which survive; for Oswald tells us less about the events than about the impression they made on him. Even his many geographic references tell us nothing about the lands he visited, except that he visited them.

II *Youthful Adventures*

Oswald was the son of Frederick von Wolkenstein, an important South Tyrolian nobleman who owned lands in the Puster Valley near Brixen and elsewhere. In marrying Katharina von Vilanders, Frederick had acquired extensive properties, including Wolkenstein Castle, which her family had bought in 1293. Oswald had two brothers: an older one, Michael, and a younger one, Leonard, as well as four sisters: Ursula, Martha, Anna, and Barbara. As we shall see, his presumed birthdate, 1377, is convincingly established by various mutually corroborating statements in his songs.

Of his earliest childhood we know almost nothing, since minors were seldom named in medieval legal and political documents; but we know that he lost an eye early in life, purportedly in a Mardi Gras accident in his seventh year. For the second decade of his life we must consult his famous autobiographical song, a song of reflection composed, as he tells us, in his thirty-eighth year. It begins:

Es fuogt sich, do ich was von zehen jaren alt,
ich wolt besehen, wie die werlt wer gestalt.
Mit ellend, armuot mangen winkel, haiss und kalt,
hab ich gebawt bei cristen, Kriechen, haiden.
Drei pfenning in dem peutel und ain stücklin brot,
das was von haim mein zerung, do ich loff in not.
Von fremden, freunden so hab ich manchen tropfen rot
gelassen seider, das ich wand verschaiden.
Ich loff ze fuoss mit swerer buoss, bis das mir starb

mein vatter zwar, wol vierzen jar, nie ross erwarb,
wan aines roupt, stal ich halbs zu mal mit valber varb
und des geleich schied ich da von mit laide.
Zwar renner, koch so was ich doch und marstaller,
auch an dem ruoder zoch ich zu mir, das was swer,
in Kandia und anderswo, ouch widerhar,
vil manchen kittel was mein bestes klaide.

When I was ten years old, it happened that I wished to see what the world was like. With misery and poverty, I dwelled in many hot and cold corners among Christians, Greeks, and heathens. Three pennies in my purse and a crust of bread, that was my sustinance when I ran away from home in hardship. Since then I have left many a red drop among strangers and kinsmen, until I thought I would perish. I journeyed on foot with great penance for fully fourteen years until my father died. I never acquired a horse, except for a fallow one I seized, or halfway stole, and immediately lost again with great sorrow. To be sure, I was a courier, cook, stable boy and also pulled a heavy oar in Candia and elsewhere and back again. Often a smock was my best garment.

Later on, we shall see that we cannot take this song to constitute a literal account of Oswald's life; since, as Ulrich Müller has amply demonstrated, he took the poetic license of interpreting some of his experiences in accordance with traditional literary topoi. However, since the factual details seem substantiated by his other songs and elsewhere, we shall for the present accept most of them at their face value. Recalling his youthful departure from home nearly thirty years later, Oswald remembers himself as a runaway; but it was more likely that he had been entrusted as a page to some knight, probably a kinsman or friend of the family, in order to learn the knightly profession. Ten was a tender age, and most boys were at least twelve or more years old before being sent out; yet it was possible for a ten-year-old to go out into the world. Eberhard Windeck, Emperor Sigismund's historian, did so in 1393 at the age of eleven; and Johannes Schiltberger, the author of one of the most interesting travelogues of Wolkenstein's day, set out in 1394 at the age of fourteen.

The term "among Christians, Greeks, and heathens" was a commonplace one, used elsewhere by Oswald (23/133) and meaning "the whole world"; because the known world of the time was inhabited only by Roman Catholics, Greek Orthodox believers, Mohammedans, and the few remaining heathens near the Baltic coast. The three pennies and the crust of bread may be expressions meaning "very little," or else they may represent some symbolic gift offered to a departing person as a good luck charm. The horse Oswald stole may have really been a fallow *(valb)*, but it is also possible that he merely remembered it as being that color, which was traditional for fine horses and also for symbolic ones like the pale horse in Revelations. It is not certain that Oswald's horse was stolen; because the words *des geleich* can mean "right away" as well as "in the same manner," that is, by theft. In a later song we shall see that, also in his youth, Oswald lost a horse when it broke its neck plunging with him down a cellar stairs. The various difficult and dirty chores Oswald performed as courier, cook, and groom were normal services demanded of a page, but only by his noble master. Pulling an oar at Candia on Crete must refer to some later adventures reported in the next strophe:

Gen Preussen, Littwan, Tartarei, Turkei, über mer, a
gen Frankreich Lampart, Ispanien mit zwaien kunges her a
traib mich die minn auf meines aigen geldes wer; a
Ruprecht, Sigmund, baid mit des adlers streiffen. b
Franzoisch, mörisch, katlonisch und kastilian, c
teutsch, latein, windisch, lampertisch, reuschisch und roman, c
die zehen sprach hab ich gebraucht, wenn mir zerran; c
auch kund ich fidlen, trummen, paugken, pfeiffen. b
Ich hab umbfarn insel und arm, manig land, ffd
auff scheffen gros, der ich genos von sturmes band, ggd
des hoch und nider meres gelider vast berant; hhd
die swarzen see lert mich ain vas begreiffen b
do mir zerbrach mit ungemach mein wargatein. iie
Ain koufman was ich, doch genas ich und kom hin, jje
ich und ain Reuss; in dem gestreuss houbguot, gewin kke
das suocht den grund und swam ich zu dem reiffen. b

Love drove me, as a self-supporting knight, toward Prussia, Lithuania, Tartary, Turkey, across the sea, and toward France, and also to Lombardy and Spain with two kings' armies: Ruprecht and Sigismund, both with the eagle pennants. French, Moorish, Catalan, and Castilian, German, Latin, Wendish, Lombard, Russian, and Romansch—those ten languages I used when it was necessary. I could also play the fiddle, trumpet, drum, and pipes. I have sailed around islands, arms of the sea, and many lands on great ships that saved me from storms; and I have sailed the high seas and the low. The Black Sea taught me to cling to a barrel, when my cargo ship broke so calamitously. I was a merchant; yet I survived and came back, I and a Russian. In the turmoil both capital and profit sought the bottom; and I swam ashore.

Whereas Oswald's earliest adventures may have occurred while he was in someone else's employment, he later traveled at his own expense *(auf meines aigen geldes wer)*. The sequence of the countries named in Oswald's list has led people to assume that his wanderings first took him to the Baltic region. Until the thirteenth century, the area later called East Prussia had been inhabited by a heathen Balto-Slavonic people called the Prussians. When the failure of the Third Crusade dimmed hope of recovering the Holy Land, the enthusiasm for converting the heathens was diverted to the northeast of Germany, where crusades won not only more souls for Jesus but also more lands for the crusaders. This *Drang nach dem Osten,* or drive toward the east, was spearheaded by the Teutonic Knights *(Deutschordens-Ritter)*, a German order of chivalry first founded for service in Palestine.

Whereas the conquest of Prussia had started with high ideals and great enthusiasm, it rapidly degenerated into a land-grab; and knights from all Western Christendom flocked to Prussia in order to win their spurs, serve the Virgin Mary, and gain their share of glory and plunder. This custom was so widespread that even Chaucer's very perfect gentle knight, who was the very model of a chivalrous gentleman, included "Pruce" among the lands he visited. By the time Oswald reached Prussia, the so-called crusades there had lost almost all religious and military significance. This had already been true in the year of his birth, when Duke Albrecht of Austria led a much publicized crusade against the Lithuanians. Despite the lavish descriptions which the poet Peter Suchenwirt gave of Albrecht's reception, hospitality, and glorious departure against the enemy, the campaign offered little action and no danger. These crusades usually followed a standard pattern: awarding of religious decorations, vigil, and prayer, and then a short and enjoyable foray against the nearly defenseless natives. Such forays quickly degenerated into a pursuit of plunder, booty, and rape, of which the first two were soon in short supply. By the time the Prussians were exterminated and the Lithuanians converted to Christianity, the religious pretext vanished entirely; and by 1410 the Teutonic Knights were defeated by the Poles and Christianized Lithuanians at Tannenberg. By this time, however, Oswald was already in Palestine, not as a crusader but as a pilgrim.

Oswald's name is not mentioned in any surviving documents of the Teutonic Knights, but this signifies little if he was still a youngster in some knight's service. Although he does not indicate where he went after leaving Lithuania, it is reasonable to suppose that he passed through Russia to the Crimea, which he called Tartary; for another of his songs lists *Reussen* and *Preussen* together (44/7). It is, of course, possible that he went more than once to Prussia, where the campaigns were usually of short duration and where the visiting knights did not like to remain for the long and cheerless winter. The last-mentioned song relates that Oswald went through *Reussen, Preussen, Eiffenlant, gen Litto, Liffen, ubern strant, gen Tennmarckh, Sweden, in Prabant, durch Flandern, Franckreich, Engelant und Schottenland.* Here the sequence is complicated, since he goes from Russia to Prussia, then up to Estonia *(Eiffenlant)*, Lithuania *(Litto)*, Livland *(Liffen)*, across the Nähringer Haff *(strant)*, and then on to Denmark. If this reflects an actual journey, he was no doubt travelling on a ship of the Hanseatic League, which then monopolized the carrying trade of the Baltic. We have no record of any early visit to Scotland or England; but, as we shall see, Oswald had good reason to visit these countries in the year 1415.

When Oswald claims that he spoke Wendish, he may have meant that he could make himself understood in various Slavonic languages, the nearest of which was Slovenian, a tongue spoken not far from his home. He also must have come into contact with various Czechs, Poles, and Wends in his journeys to the Baltic; and it should be remembered that Wendish was then spoken on most of the southern coast of the Baltic and even in spots west of the Elbe River. By Lombard, Oswald meant northern Italian; which was quite distinct from Sicilian and was the first Romance dialect he encountered in going south from his Tyrolian homeland. There being no evidence or likelihood that he ever sojourned for long in Romania, the *Roman* that he spoke was surely Romansch or Ladinsch, the Latin dialect still spoken in the Dolomites and in the immediate vicinity of Wolkenstein. Although Oswald lists only ten languages, he could have listed twelve; since he also composed a song in Flemish, *Grasselick Lif* (96), and mixed a few Flemish and Magyar crumbs in his polyglot song *Do fraig amors* (69). Nevertheless, we may be sure that his knowledge of some of these tongues would have offended a purist.

The anecdote about the shipwreck in the Black Sea will be discussed at length later. Since it is unlikely that Oswald would have acquired enough experience and capital to undertake a commercial venture by himself, it is probable that he was serving as an armed escort for some Russian merchant, possibly one carrying furs down the Don or Dnieper and across the Black Sea to Turkey or Byzantium. His expression "across the sea" *(über mer)* was a standing term for "in Palestine," just as the World War I expressions, "overseas" and "over there" meant "in France." Since Oswald's pilgrimage is better known than his other early adventures, it will be discussed separately.

We know much about Oswald's trip to Spain with Sigismund, but little about his earlier trip with Ruprecht to Lombardy. His youthful travels had occurred during the reign of "Lazy Wenzel" (1387–1400), a namesake of our "Good King Wenceslaus". On August 20, 1400, the prince electors deposed Wenzel as king of the Holy Roman Empire and elected Ruprecht, the Rhinegrave of the Palatinate, who was crowned in Cologne on January 6, 1401. Ruprecht was king, but he could not assume the title of emperor until being crowned by the pope in Rome. This he tried to accomplish that same year, but without success; for, in passing through Lombardy, he was defeated by the Milanese duke, Gian Galeazzo Visconti, who prevented him from completing his journey. As will be shown, Oswald was most frequently on the losing side.

Ruprecht was the father of Rhinegrave Ludwig III, who became a close friend of Oswald. Being the count of the Rhenish Palatinate *(Rheinpfalz)*, or the region around Heidelberg, Ludwig was called both Rhinegrave *(Rheingraf)* and Count Palatine *(Pfalzgraf)*. Ruprecht was followed as "Roman King" by Sigismund, the king of Hungary, whom we will call "Emperor" to indicate his function as head of the Holy Roman Empire, even though he remained officially "Roman King" from his election in 1410 until his coronation in Rome in 1433.

As Oswald mentions in his farewell to youth *(Es fuogt sich)*, he had no horse until his father died. That seems to have happened in 1401; yet Oswald did not receive his inheritance until his older brother divided the property some time later. Michael, who had married in 1401, did not wish to distribute the family inheritance until the youngest brother, Leonhard, had come of age; and Oswald grew impatient. One day, while Michael and his wife were away from home, Oswald stole a chest of jewels and then tried to evade blame by accusing his sister-in-law of having misappropriated them with the help of her lover. Luckily for Michael, he found the jewels at a jeweler's, to whom Leonhard had brought them to be altered. On another occasion Oswald tried to purloin some rents due to Michael, and this led to a bloody fight in which Michael thrust a sword into Oswald and forced him to confess to having falsely maligned his wife. This "dark point" in Oswald's life, as it was called by Anton Noggler, explains Oswald's statement that he had shed blood "among strangers and kinsmen"; and it may be alluded to in another of Oswald's songs of reminiscence (23/57–64), which will be discussed later. Scholars formerly thought that *fremden freunden* was an oxymoron: "strange friends," but now it is generally accepted as an antithesis: "strangers, kinsmen," since Oswald often used antitheses, for example the reference to *Ruprecht, Sigmund* in the same song (18/20).

Michael at last divided his father's property on April 22, 1407, thus creating three separate Wolkenstein dynasties: the Wolkenstein-Trostburgs, descended from Michael; the Wolkenstein-Rodeneggs, descended from Oswald; and the Wolkenstein-Aichachs, descended from Leonhard. Having come into his own, Oswald demonstrated his piety, and vanity, by dedicating a chapel at Brixen to his patron, St. Oswald, who had saved him in his Black Sea shipwreck. To celebrate his rescue, Oswald decorated his chapel with a now lost mural of himself clinging to a barrel. Then, in order to perpetuate his fame still further, he also adorned the chapel with an almost life-sized bas-relief of himself. This monument, which was eventually lost from sight and immured, was rediscovered in 1847, just four years before Beda Weber published Oswald's songs. It is now mounted on a wall of the cloister at Brixen.

Because Oswald is wearing a long beard in the bas-relief, it seems likely that he was already planning his pilgrimage when it was carved; for a long beard was as much a part of the pilgrim's costume as was the cowl (*kutten*, 18/56), which Oswald also describes as a *kappen mit dem lappen* (18/58). Although his beard was already long in the bas-relief of 1408, there is evidence that he did not make the pilgrimage until about 1409–1411. As Norbert Mayr has shown, there are no documents attesting his presence in Tyrol between May 25, 1409, and January 21, 1411. His songs suggest that he journeyed alone; but it is more likely that he waited to go with some group, perhaps with some great lord's retinue, for safety and economy. Some fifteen years later, Rhinegrave Ludwig invited Oswald to accompany him to the Holy Land on a large-scale expedition.

Like other pilgrims of his day, Oswald surely had varied motives for undertaking his journey, such as love of excitement, a craving for fame, and the ambition to receive the Order of the Holy Sepulcher. Even piety may have played a role. Various hints in his songs, as well as the recorded voyages of his contemporaries, suggest that he sailed from Venice, stopped at Cyprus, and landed in Syria. It is usually assumed that he returned via Tripoli, Sicily, and Naples; but this may result from a false interpretation of *Trippel in Barbarei* (12/56). Since the word *Barbarei* was then applied not only to the southern but also to the eastern coast of the Mediterranean, the name *Trippel* may designate Tripolis, a Syrian city prominent in the crusades.

While in Palestine, Oswald naturally visited the Holy Sepulcher, where he may have been initiated into the order of that name. This is suggested by one of his verses in which he says that he used to be Mary's servant but is now her knight (106/22), unless perhaps he had also become a Teutonic Knight, that order being especially dedicated to Mary. Oswald also visited Bethlehem, if we may believe a later Christmas song, which says that he saw that town (126/5–12). He also claims to have seen the cleft in the rock which the devil made in his anger at the birth of Jesus (35/12). It is a moot question whether he made the dangerous excursion to the cloister of St. Catherine in the Sinai Desert; but this is entirely possible, since she was one of the very few saints whom he later invoked (1/9).

III *Sabina Songs*

It is generally supposed that the lady in whose service Oswald made his pilgrimage was the daughter of Martin Jäger, part owner of the Hauenstein estate near Kastelruth, of which Frederick von Wolkenstein had inherited a share from the Vilanders. The Jägers and the Vilanders had fought for Hauenstein for many years, even after the bishop of Brixen had arbitrated in 1397 and awarded two-thirds of the joint ownership to the Jägers and one third to the Wolkensteins. Unfortunately for Oswald, the Wolkenstein claim to the Hauenstein estate fell to him in the division of the inheritance and continued to be an "albatross around his neck."

According to Weber, Martin Jäger's daughter was named Sabina, a name that is nowhere recorded. Mayr believes that her real name was Barbara; but, since this has not been proved, we will follow the convention of using the name Sabina to designate the *femme fatale* in Oswald's life. Weber reports that Sabina rid herself of her impetuous suitor by sending him to the Holy Land, from which he returned only to find her married to Hans Hausman, a rich old burgher of Brixen. Mayr produces convincing evidence to show that Sabina was already married to Hausman when Oswald first met her and that Weber's entire romance stemmed from his personal interpretation of the few facts given in Oswald's songs, yet this myth of the perfidious fiancée clings tenaciously. It is only natural to suppose that Oswald met Sabina in 1407, at which time they became co-heirs of the Hauenstein estates.

That Oswald had met Sabina by 1408 seems confirmed by his song *Ain anefangk,* which seems to have been composed in 1421; for it claims that he has been true to her *wol dreuzen jar und dennocht mer* (for thirteen years and more, 1/21).[2] This was apparently the year in which Sabina became a wife and also a widow; and it was one year after Oswald inherited his claim to a part of her Hauenstein property. This does not suggest that Oswald was courting Sabina in order to acquire Hauenstein; for the Jägers were a modest family and hardly wealthy enough to arouse Oswald's marital interests. When Oswald finally married, it was for far greater stakes, even though, as he attested, he was still enamored of Sabina. On May 25, 1409, Oswald was appointed

Hauptmann des Gotteshauses, or captain of the cloister, at Brixen, so that he remained Sabina's neighbor.

In the fourth strophe of his farewell to youth, Oswald reports that he sought out tournaments in the service of a lady but that he did not wish to reveal the affair (*Die weil ich rait und suochet ritterliche spil und dient zu willen ainer frauen, des ich hil,* 18/54). Although he was obeying the mandate of *taugenminne* (secret love), that is to say, the Chesterfieldian policy of never mentioning a lady's name, it has been generally assumed that he was referring to Sabina, whose name appears only once in all his songs, and then only after her death. Even in this case, however, he uses her married name, *die Hausmanin* (26/120).

The fifth strophe of the song is entirely devoted to Oswald's hopeless passion for this woman. He begins by saying that it would take too long to tell of all his sorrow; but then he proceeds to do so after all, starting with the amorous convention that he has been wounded to death by a choice red mouth. Next follows a clinical diagnosis of the symptoms of such a malady: sweating, blushing, turning pale, trembling, sighing, oblivion of his own body, and vain attempts to escape his passion by seeking refuge in hardships and exile. Such a slick résumé of all the Ovidian clichés certainly suggests more playfulness than passion, but we shall save the problem of autobiographical authenticity until later.

If we accept Oswald's claim that this was the one passion of his youth, we can attribute all his early love lyrics to Sabina, assuming, of course, that they were based on actual experience. But this is of little use, because we do not know which of his love lyrics are early ones and can only speculate about their dates. We shall, therefore, limit ourselves, at this time, to discussing several songs which seem, for various reasons, to have been written to or about the lady. Probably the earliest of these is a charming little song beginning *Ain mensch von achzehen jaren kluog.* If this song was written early in their acquaintance, say in 1407 or 1408, Sabina must have been born in 1389 or 1390. In this song Oswald states that, having only one eye, he simply cannot see enough of her; and again we hear that her red mouth has conquered him and allows him no rest. Even when he has journeyed far away, he asserts, her fair face appears to him and her tender glances seize his heart. No other girl was ever so womanly, her beautiful demeanor *(gepärd)* robs him of his comfort, especially when he thinks of her perfect measurements.

Life with this young lady was never dull, as we learn from a song beginning *Mein buol laisst mir gesellschafft zwar*. The girl accompanies him just as the months do the year. Sometimes she is as cold as January and February; and sometimes she makes him sick and well with pleasure and pain, just as doctors say that March does. She is as fickle as April, as beautiful as May, and as colorful as June. July has made her breasts and arms so white and her hands so smooth; and she is as well turned as the pears that ripen in August. Sometimes she discourages him like September, yet he hopes that October will bring him a harvest of luck. November also provides nourishment; but December is cold both day and night. Although Oswald had to stretch facts and logic in order to accommodate all the months to his pattern, he has done so most adroitly; and the song suggests the months as illustrated in such books as the *Book of the Hours* of the Duc de Berry. The song is less artless than it first appears: for example, Oswald consciously uses chiasmus in saying that pleasure and pain made him sick and well, since the sequence of *lieb* and *laid* was not required by the rhyme.

Another *Loblied* (song of praise), probably also addressed to Sabina, explains the allusion to the pears in the previous song. This song, beginning *Du ausserweltes schöns mein herz,* likewise tells how his chosen beauty can take away his sorrow and how he has not lost hope, even though parting brings sour sugar. In describing her charms, Oswald boasts that her white breasts are as round as pears; and in this he is following a masculine convention that still survives in Austria, where men categorize women's breasts as either apples or pears. To judge by the miniatures in thirteenth-century songbooks, it would seem that the men of that idealistic period actually envisaged women's breasts as being round like apples. On the other hand, Wolkenstein's more realistic contemporaries seemed to realize that apple breasts owe less to physique than to foundation garments. If the bodice is less tightly laced, the breasts do not stand straight out but appear to be suspended from the chest above; and thus they resemble pears rather than apples. It will be noted that Oswald always likened breasts to pears, never to apples.

This three-voiced song is not one of Oswald's best; but it differs from any that preceded it. When he compares his sweetheart to a tercel (a male falcon!), he elaborates the image by referring to her sweet little beak. He also expresses the time-worn oxymoron about the delightful agony or painful pleasure of love with a new twist by saying that yearning parting brings sour sugar. The term "yearning parting" (*sennliches schaiden,* 46/14) is typically Oswaldian, a telegraphic way of implying that the separation will cause future yearning. The use of a concrete word like "sugar" in place of the abstract word "sweetness" is typical of Oswald's tendency to appeal to the senses rather than the intellect; for he was a poet of sound, sight, scent, touch, and taste.

In his farewell to youth (18/55), Oswald relates that his lady-love would not accept his service until he wore a pilgrim's cowl for two years. The resulting pilgrimage, which he seems to have made between 1409 and 1411, was a high point in his life and furnished much matter for reminiscence. From it comes the song *Var, heng, und lass,* an *Abschiedslied,* or song of parting, in which a youth takes leave of the damsel who has sent him on his pilgrimage. For unexplained reasons, it is the girl who instructs her lover how to sail, which winds to use, and which to avoid. The most interesting thing about the song is the nautical terminology used in describing the several winds and the art of sailing. Since these terms do not match any specific Italian dialect, it was long believed that Oswald created them for the sake of their rhymes and sound effects, until Mayr proved that they were good phonetic transcriptions of the nautical jargon or maritime koiné used by various Italian sailors on the Adriatic and Mediterranean.

It is to be noted that the winds are listed in the order in which they appear on the compass card. It is generally believed that the song was composed on the return journey, after Oswald had lost his devotion and shaken off his cowl (*do ich die kutt mit andacht schutt,* 18/62). I believe, however, that it was composed on the way to Palestine; because Oswald states that they should *orzen* (17/28), or sail with the wind from the left. Since the wind in question is the *grego,* or northeast wind, they would have to be sailing southeast, or in the direction to, not from, Palestine. This song, which Oswald composed when he was about thirty-nine years old, is the earliest that can be dated with any degree of certainty. He must have composed it on the voyage, and not from recollection, since the only people who could have understood and appreciated it were his fellow travelers who were familiar with the same nautical terms.

That Oswald's pilgrimage was allegedly a love service is indicated in one other song, namely the one beginning *Ach senliches leiden.* The first strophe is cited to show what intricate rhyme schemes Oswald sometimes affected:

Ach senliches leiden, a
meiden, neiden, schaiden, das tuot we; aaab
besser wer versunken in dem see. b
Zart minnikliches weib, c
dein leib mich schreibt und treibt gen Josophat. cccd
Herz, muot, sin, gedanck ist worden mat. d
Es schaidt der tod, e
ob mir dein gnad nicht helfen wil df
auss grosser not. e
Mein angst ich dir verhil. f
Dein mündlin rot e
hat mir so schier mein gier erwecket vil, gggf
des wart ich genaden an dem zil. f

Alas, love-pains, avoidance, jealousy, parting: all that causes pain. It would be better to be sunk in the sea. Tender lovely girl, you exile and drive me toward Josaphat. My heart, spirit, mind, and thoughts are faint. Death will release me if your mercy will not help me. I conceal my fear from you. Your red mouth has aroused my desire so keenly that I am waiting for ultimate mercy.

The name Josophat is taken to refer to the Valley of Jehoshaphat, the valley of the Kidron in Palestine, in which case the song must have been composed while Oswald was still on his way there.[3] In this song, Oswald has produced one very vivid image by saying that, while exiled from his love, he is waiting like the dolphin that has fled from the storm and remains in the depths of the sea until it can finally emerge into the bright day to be refreshed by the brilliance of the sun.

Proof that Oswald considered his Palestinian pilgrimage one of his great accomplishments is seen in his dedicating an entire strophe to it some five years later in his farewell to youth. There he relates:

I wanted to change my foolish life, that is the truth, and became half-way a beghard for two whole years. To be sure, it all began with great devotion, if only love had not disturbed the end. As long as I had ridden forth and sought tournaments and served the will of a lady, whose name I shall conceal, she had refused to show me a speck of mercy until a cowl should make a fool of me. Everything began to go smoothly when the cape and the cowl enwrapped me. Never before or afterwards has any maid who has accepted my words so lovingly been so tied up with my destiny. All of a sudden my devotion flew out through the gable when I shook off my cowl in the fog. Since then, I have suffered many a battle as pastime and all my joy has been frozen. (18/49–64)

This strophe shows that Oswald, like most fifteenth-century poets, often expressed muddled thoughts and did not try to place his ideas in any logical sequence. Regardless of what motives he really had for his pilgrimage, the reason he gives is his love service to a lady, whose name he must conceal according to the laws of chivalry. Unsatisfied with the tournaments he has fought in her service, she requires him to go to Palestine as a proof of his devotion. Oswald seems to contradict himself, and we are never sure whether the pilgrimage was due to religious or amorous devotion. The term "beghard" referred specifically to a mendicant order in the Low Countries, and by extension to any vagabond or beggar.

IV *The "Last Minnesinger"*

Nineteenth-century scholars often called Oswald "the last minnesinger," but with little justification. In conformity with the idealism of their age, the provençal troubadours and German minnesingers of the High Middle Ages had evolved a theory of selfless and sublimated love *(fin amor, hôhiu minne)* in which the lover adored his beloved without hope of requital. As we shall see, such a "vegetable" passion was incomprehensible to Wolkenstein, for whom love, like food and drink, was a physical necessity. Consequently, although he followed in the footsteps of the minnesingers and even used similar motifs and poetic forms, he usually filled them with new content.

Many theories have been proposed to explain the sudden adoration of women in the twelfth century. Origins have been found in Latin panegyrics, in a secularization of mystical divine love, in literary practices of the Spanish Moors, in a transferral of the veneration of the Virgin Mary to earthly women, and in many other precedents. But, regardless of how significantly courtly love was influenced by any or all of these factors, it is clear that it was expressed largely in feudal terms. A vassal owed unswerving loyalty to his lord and, by extension, to his lord's lady. Just as a vassal could uphold his lord's honor by fighting for him in battles or tournaments, he could serve his lady with feats of arms. If he was a gifted singer, he could also serve her by singing her praises, thus spreading her fame.

Since service to a lady paralleled service to a lord, the terminology of feudalism well suited the new love service. That is to say, the language of *herrendienst,* or service to one's lord, was easily adapted to *frouwendienst,* or service to one's lady. The beloved was the knight's lady *(frouwe),* as he was her servitor *(dienstman).* He served her with loyalty *(triuwe)* and constancy *(stæte),* and she rewarded him with her mercy *(genâde)* or favor *(huld).* As the wife of the lord, she could not requite her servitor's love, which could never be consummated; but she was expected to accept and recognize his service. If she did not, then she was *ungenædig,* ungracious or *sans merci,* and therefore an ungrateful wretch in danger of losing her womanly honor. In addition to the feudal terminology, the minnesingers transferred many terms from the art of war to the art of love; for, as Ovid had noted, every lover is a soldier *(militat omnis amans).* Thus, the lady's beauty is a sword or spear that wounds the lover's heart, and he is quickly conquered *(betwungen)* or captured *(gefangen).*

There were several virtues dear to the minnesingers that Oswald did not stress. Among these was *milde,* or largesse, a virtue greatly emphasized by the mendicant minnesingers, but Oswald required no patron and usually sang as a peer among peers. Nor did he stress the value of *mâze,* or moderation; for moderation and temperance were foreign to his nature and to the turbulent age that shaped him. Like the minnesingers, he praised *zuht,* or good breeding; but he used the term only to refer to proper womanly behavior. The courtly narrators had been fond of the word *verligen,* meaning to be indolent; but Oswald used it only once. Whereas the minnesingers had frequently used the term *hôher muot* to designate the high spirits and affirmative outlook proper for courtiers, especially the kind inspired by beautiful ladies, Oswald used it seldom and usually in a comical or parodistic context, as, for example, when it denotes the joy a full purse can give a woman (25/6). *Hochvart,* which had once designated noble demeanor, appears in Oswald's songs only as *hoffart,* the Christian sin of pride (4/15).

Although Oswald rejected, or perhaps did not inherit, some of the minnesingers' vocabulary, he did make good use of much of it. Typical is his *Dienstlied* (servitor's song) beginning *Herz, muot, leib, sel und was ich han,* in which he declares that he is the subject *(undertan)* of a fair face whom he has resolved to serve with constancy *(stetiklich).* He swears that he will never forget her and that no emperor would be his equal if she were to remember him. He wishes that she knew even half the love he bears for her; for she brings him more joy than any other woman. No matter how far away he is, her proud *leib* appears to him *inbrünstiklich* and excites his *senlich* desires. It is not clear just how we are to understand these words. The classic minnesingers used the word *leib (lîp)* to denote the whole person—soul and mind as well as body—as in the English words "somebody" and "anybody" and in the verse "If a body meet a body coming through the Rye." It will be noted that Oswald used the word *leib* in this general sense in verse 5 of the above-quoted strophe beginning *Ach senliches leiden;* but in the present song it seems to connote primarily the physical aspect of the woman. The word *inbrünstiklich* (ardently) is surely a transferred epithet, since he, rather than she, is the one showing the ardor. To judge by some of Oswald's other songs, we might suppose that the *Inbrunst* he felt was really a *Brunst* (heat); for he often likened himself to animals.

Oswald composed another *Dienstlied,* beginning *Gar wunniklich,* which is unusual in that the rhyme depends entirely upon polyphony. All of its rhymes are *Körner,* a *Korn* being a word that rhymes with corresponding words in the other strophes but not with any in its own. Wolkenstein used *Körner* often, usually in the last verse of each strophe, in order to link the strophes and give unity to the song. If the last word of a verse did not rhyme, it was called a *Waise* (orphan).

Illustrative of Oswald's use of time-worn clichés is a little *Minneklage,* or lover's complaint, which has slight merit except for an unexpected twist at the end. The song, which begins *Mein herz, das ist versert,* is remarkable for neither its rhyme nor its meter; accordingly, a summary will suffice to show how Oswald used and abused traditional material. First he states that his heart is sore and twice wounded to the quick by a sharp and poisoned sword, and that there is no doctor in the world who can heal him except for the person who inflicted the injury. He then implores his lady to crown her noble nature and preserve her greatest treasure (her honor), so that her image [4] will not be damaged in scandal's snare and no tongue will find pleasure in slandering her; for then his heart will be healed and refreshed. He reminds her of her willing promise of comfort (or confidently reminds her of her promise); and he asks her to think of his pitiable death so that he will be saved. And then he adds the unexpected ending, "It is surely much better to die young with honor than to live here for two hundred years in shame."

This ending is a misapplication of another favorite commonplace of medieval literature, the maxim that death with honor is better than a life of shame. Agricola had expressed the idea as *honesta mors turpi vita potior* when haranguing his troops in Britain, where the idea was expressed nearly a millennium later by the author of *Beowulf* as *Death bith sella eorla gewhylcum thonne edwitlif*. This commonplace was, of course, always applied to a warrior who would lose his honor through cowardice, not to a woman who would lose her good name by failing to reward her faithful servant. The fact that Oswald believed that an ungrateful woman would lose her honor is attested in another song, in which he admonishes the Virgin Mary to preserve her honor by recognizing his service (12/81).

Typical of Wolkenstein's love songs is a *Loblied* beginning *Wol mich an we der lieben stund*. Like his thirteenth-century predecessors, he expresses the joy he experiences when a certain rosy mouth smiles at him; and then he describes his sweetheart's lovely face. Whereas that would have sufficed in songs of *hôhiu minne* (lofty love), Oswald further admits how much he would enjoy a kiss from her. Nor does he stop there. He next describes her beautiful breasts and declares how happy he would be to embrace her. Finally, he admits that he is really thinking of what is between her belt and her feet and that he would be overjoyed if he could grab her there and lie with her body, hands, feet, and legs. Here, the sequence of his desires is exceptional; for he usually follows the three stages of love as recommended by Andreas

Capellanus' handbook on the art of love: first the embrace, then the kiss, then the fulfillment.

Since only consummated love was worthwhile for Oswald, the minnesong genre that appealed to him most was the *tageliet,* or morning song, a song depicting the painful parting of two lovers after a night of love. The following apparently artless song shows that Oswald could compose such a *tageliet* if he wished.

Wach auff, mein hort!	es leucht dort her	wx
von orient der liechte tag.		y
Blick durch die braw,	vernim den glanz,	da
wie gar vein blaw	des himels kranz	da
sich mengt durch graw	von rechter schanz.	da
Ich furcht ain kurzlich tagen.		z
"Ich klag das mort,	des ich nicht ger,	wx
man hört die voglin in dem hag		y
mit hellem hal	erklingen schon.	eb
O nachtigal,	dein spëcher don	eb
mir pringet qual,	des ich nicht lon.	eb
Unweiplich muss ich klagen."		z
Mit urlob fort!	deins herzen sper	wx
mich wunt, seid ich nicht bleiben mag.		y
Schidliche not	mir trauren pringt,	fc
dein mündlin rot	mich senlich zwingt,	fc
der bitter tod	mich minder dringt.	fc
Mich schaiden macht verzagen.		z

Wake up, my Love! The bright day is shining forth from the east. Look through your brows, perceive the brilliance, how beautifully blue the wreath of heaven is blending with the grey in such a lovely fashion. I fear the day will soon break.

"I lament the fate which I do not desire. You can hear the birds in the hedges already singing with clear resonance. Oh, nightingale, your smart tune brings me agony that I do not deserve. It makes me weep in an unwomanly way."

With your leave, I must go! The spear of your heart is wounding me, since I can no longer remain. The pain of parting brings me sorrow, your red mouth overcomes me with yearning, bitter death would afflict me less. Parting makes me despair.

Here we encounter all the old clichés: the day breaking in the east, the lovers' fear of parting, the songs of the birds, especially of the nightingale, the heart that wounds like a spear, the red mouth that conquers the lover, and the despondency over separation. Oswald has added nothing new: in fact, a comparison with his other so-called morning songs will indicate that he was earnestly endeavoring to remain within the *tageliet* tradition. Yet he does express his traditional ideas in a novel and individual way. For example, when the lover tells his lady to "look through your brow," this suggests the efforts of a walking person to focus; for many people, when squinting, can see the edge of their eyesocket as a frame around the sight they see. This image recalls one in Gottfried Keller's *Abendlied,* when the poet requests his eyes to drink in what his eyelashes hold *(was die Wimper hält)* of the golden abundance of the world. In reading Oswald's apparently simple song one does not immediately observe the intricate rhyme scheme, in which the first two verses and the last verse of every strophe are *Körner* (represented by w, x, y, & z).

Oswald composed another morning song that more or less fits the genre as established by the troubadours and minnesingers, at least in subject matter. This song is sung by three voices, those of the two lovers and that of the watchman who awakens them with his horn. Two voices are singing simultaneously all the time, thus making a duet; but the roles change. While the woman and the watchman are taking turns during the first twelve verses, the knight is also singing his part, the verses of which rhyme with those assigned to the other two singers. In the following eight verses the roles are reversed: the knight and the watchman alternate, and their verses rhyme with those being sung simultaneously by the woman. Since two voices are singing different words at the same time, it is unlikely that the audience understood the lyrics. The woman and the watchman begin their parts as follows:

> "Sag an, herzlieb, nu was bedeutet uns so gar schrecklicher hall
> mit seinem don?"
> aahü, aahü, wol auf, die nacken bloss!
> "Ainiger man, sol uns der gast erstören hie so ach ellend?
> wem lastu mich?"
> aahü, aahü, her gat des tages schein. . . .

"Tell me, dear heart, what does that frightful resounding mean with its noise?" Ahoo, ahoo. Get up, bare your necks . . . "Beloved man, should the stranger disturb us here so miserably? To whom are you leaving me?" Ahoo, ahoo, the brightness of the day is approaching. . . .

The watchman continues his song, warning all lovers that it is time to part; for the birds are singing in the woods. This time it is not just the nightingale—the bird so dear to the minnesingers—but also the blackbird, thrush, finch, and a siskin that calls himself *guggukh.* The *aahü,* which represents the sound of the watchman's horn, was probably produced by an accompanying horn.

In the second strophe of the above song we find the repetition of the rhyme *-ent* four times in close proximity: *orient, entrennt, blennt,* and *firmament.* Oswald used this rhyme even more spectacularly in a morning song beginning *Es seusst dort her von orient,* in which the first fourteen verses end with it. A fifteenth verse, ending with *geschlĕchte,* is followed by fourteen verses rhyming on *art,* which, in turn, are followed by a verse ending with *geträchte.* Since Oswald had to force two more strophes into this intricate rhyme scheme, as well as having to supply each with an even more elaborate refrain including both terminal and initial rhyme, we can be sure that he was more concerned with the rhymes than with the meaning.

The most novel thing about the song discussed above is Wolkenstein's use of the east wind as a harbinger of the day. This motif appears again in an even more complicated morning song beginning *Ich spür ain lufft aus küelem tufft,* which likewise consists of three long strophes each followed by a refrain. In observing Oswald's elaborate use of rhymes in such songs, we must marvel at his virtuosity while regretting his lack of (twentieth-century) taste. Whereas the previous song had mentioned blackbirds, thrushes, finches, and a siskin, this one mentions crested larks, skylarks, siskins, thrushes, and nightingales. Thus we see Oswald using the rhetorical device of *accumulatio,* or a heaping up of words as a verbal adornment.

Whereas all these songs can be classified as morning songs, at least in subject matter, Oswald composed many other songs that are often called such, even though they actually share only a few of the outer trimmings of the genre. Sometimes, for example in the song *Erwach an schrick, vil schönes weib,* the lovers awaken, not to part with sorrow, but to arise and join the May-dance. But this introduces another favorite genre of the minnesingers, the May song, which Oswald adopted often, but always in his own peculiar way.

The winters in Central Europe, especially in the Alps, are long and cold; and medieval people had no central heating, no fresh food, and little entertainment during the long winter months. Even the castles were dank and dreary, being built for protection rather than warmth and comfort; thus it is understandable that people, like animals, longed for the warm rays of the sun. The heathen Germans had welcomed summer with fertility rites, which included songs, dances, and pantomimes. With the introduction of Christianity, these rituals lost their religious significance; yet they remained popular as an occasion for public merriment. To celebrate such festive events, Oswald composed numerous lively dance songs.

May songs *(Mailieder)* were also called summer songs *(Sommerlieder)*, the words for May and summer being practically synonymous at the time. All of these songs are composed to accompany the dancing; and, consequently, the ideas, to which the dancers paid little attention, are inconsequential. At times there seems to be no train of thought at all, or at least the syntax is occasionally muddled. Typical of these is a song of four strophes, the first of which will be cited to indicate the rhythm and rhyme scheme. No translation is given, because the thoughts hardly merit one:

Nempt war der schönen plüede, früede!	aa
müede ist der kalde winder.	ab
Kinder, schickt eu zu dem tanz!	bc
glanz zieret sich lustlich des maien tenne	cd
durch manger hendlin farbe, garbe,	ee
marbe würzlin, grüene gräsli,	ef
wäsli mit den plüemlin gel.	fg
Hel singt die nachtigal weit für die henne.	gd
Die droschel hat ein wett getan	h
mit ainem alten rappen	i
zu tichten auff des maien pan,	h
und gilt ain junge kappen.	i
Vil stolzer maide wellen dran,	h
das wiss, ir röschen knappen.	i

Although specific details are unusual in summer songs, in the third strophe of this song the singer assures his beloved, in whose service he is, that he has served her for eight years (106/37). If this song is autobiographic and refers to Sabina, it can hardly have been composed before 1415.

Even more compelling is the rhythm of a still longer dance song beginning:

Vil lieber grüesse   süesse   aa
sich erheben,   streben,   bb
frölich,   zölich,   jetten   ccd
tretten   in das phat.   de
Drat   fruo und spat   ee
hört man dringen,   f
singen,   klingen   ff
voglin in der auen,   g
durch helle döne   schöne,   hh
in den strauchen   rauhen,   ii
esten   glesten, fliegen,   jjk
kriegen   widerstreit.   kl
Breit   angerweit   ll
sol man grüenlich,   m
küenlich,   süenlich,   mm
kurlich ane schauen.   n
Winder kalt,   o
ungestalt,   o
dein gewalt   o
ist entspalt   o
von den süessen lüfften.   p
Liechten summer   q
ane kummer   q
wil ich tummer   q
also ain frummer   q
geuden und güffte.   p
Grüener kle   r
jagt den snee   r
jarlang me   r
inn den see   r
wilder mere flüete.   s
Nachtigalle,   t
droschel schalle,   t
lerchen halle   t
uns gevalle   t
für des ofens güete.   s

The irresistible rhythm of this song suggests that of Poe's "The Bells." Less elaborate and impelling is another dance song beginning *Des himels trone,* in which the syntax is sometimes so loose that any punctuation is fanciful. An even more original use of language is found in a rollicking dance song beginning *Frölich, zärtlich.* This song starts as a morning song but immediately becomes an invitation to the dance; and it finally turns out to have been only a daydream, or one might say an erotic reverie. It has been sensitively analyzed by Frank Banta.[5]

All these dance songs share the same restricted requisites: melting snow, sprouting flowers and grass, singing birds, pretty lasses, and amorous lads. One of them, beginning *Der mai mit lieber zal,* presents all the little birds, each with its own song. Oswald seems to have missed, or forgotten, the point of his source, a virelay composed by Jehan Vaillant of Paris about 1370. The little birds in Vaillant's song are holding court to try the cuckoo for his crimes. When Oswald's birds sing *oci, oci* and *tu, tu,* they are only talking bird-talk, whereas Vaillant's birds are speaking French and saying "Kill, kill!" But even without any plot Oswald's ornithological medley is quite charming as reproduced on the phonograph recording of his songs produced by the Deutsche Grammophongesellschaft.[6] Some of the best of Oswald's summer songs, such as *Wol auff, wol an!,* were written for his wife and therefore belong to another section of this study.

V *Neidhart Songs*

Like other minnesingers, Walther had favored May dances, but only as long as they observed good decorum and were without any rusticity *(âne alle dörperheit).* But even fine lords and gentle ladies sometimes abandoned themselves to the excitement of the May dance, which, unlike the imported French courtly dances, were partially of native peasant origin. Although the courtier Walther had introduced songs of natural love involving peasant girls, he resented the intrusion of rustic melodies at court, as he complains in his sarcastic song *Ouwê hovelîches singen.* This bitter diatribe may well have been aimed at Neidhart of Reuental, a court singer whose rustic dance songs sometimes showed him competing with peasant swains for the village belles at the dance. German scholars have named such songs *höfische Dorfpoesie* (courtly village poetry); but they should have called them "rustic court poetry," since they were composed for courtiers rather than for villagers. (Actually, they should be called "songs," not "poems," since the lyrics were never performed without the music.) Neidhart songs became popular at court despite all that Walther and other arbiters of good taste could do; and they maintained their popularity until Oswald's time. Oswald himself was familiar with them and mentions Neidhart in one of his songs (9/37, unless in this context Neidhart means an envious person).

In a self-commiserating song written in his later years while under virtual house arrest at Hauenstein Castle, Oswald complained that, after having enjoyed the refinements of the gayest capitals of Europe, he was then rusticating in a rural milieu. No matter where he looked, he could see nothing but calves, goats, cattle, and coarse, dark, ugly people (44/46). That would have been true of Oswald whenever he was living on his own property; for most of his castles were remote from courtly life, especially during the long snowbound winters. It is probable that he saw no cultivated people for months at a time, except for his immediate family, his scribe and steward, and perhaps an occasional guest. Consequently, he must have had far more social intercourse (and perhaps sexual as well) with the peasantry than the courtly poets would have recommended.

In his *Germania* of A.D. 98, the Roman historian Tacitus had noted that the Germanic children played together regardless of social class until natural virtue separated the wellborn from the rest; and we may be sure that this long continued to be the case among the rural nobility in the lands occupied by their descendants. Noble children in isolated castles would have no other playmates until they were sent off as pages to learn their manners, and social prejudices, at some larger court, just as the sons of planters in the antebellum South played with the slave children until being sent off to school to learn good manners and racial superiority.

Oswald's rustic songs contain many words not found in any dictionaries. They are obviously subliterary ones missing from such compilations because these rely on literary sources. Being nonliterary, some of these words may have been found only in Oswald's South Tyrolian dialect, or at best in the general Bavarian dialect of which it is a subdivision. Typical of Oswald's Neidhart songs is a combination of drinking and dancing song beginning:

Her wiert, uns durstet also sere,			a
trag auf wein!	trag auf wein!	trag auf wein!	bbb
Das dir got dein laid verkere,			a
pring her wein!	pring her wein!	pring her wein!	bbb
und dir dein salden mere,			a
nu schenck ein!	nu schenck ein!	nu schenck ein!	bbb

Sir host, we are so very thirsty, serve us wine, serve us wine, serve us wine. So that God will divert your sorrow, bring us wine, bring us wine, bring us wine. And so that He will increase your joys, pour me mine, pour me mine, pour me mine.

It is easy to visualize the *Vorsänger,* or solo voice, intoning the first, third, and fifth verses, while his fellow carousers join in the refrains. The peasant element, including obscenity, is first introduced in the second strophe; and the remaining four strophes abound in traditional Neidhart humor, not the least of which was the accumulation of peasant names and the description of boisterous and rowdy dancing.

Perhaps Oswald's most extensive use of boorish language is found in *Got geb eu ainen guoten morgen,* a dialogue between a love-struck swain and an indifferent woman. The youth addresses his beloved as "very noble empress," but she answers that she already has a sweetheart living in Kastelruth. Despite his many adulations and entreaties, she continues to swear undying devotion to her true love; and she finally rids herself of her impetuous suitor by sending him off to chop, thresh, dig, mow, and plow. The song contains many words not found in Oswald's more urbane songs, such as *neut* for *nicht, brechten* and *keuen* for *sprechen, numerdum* for *in nomine domini,* and *versorten* for *verflucht.* In addition, there are many rhyme pairs which do not appear in most of the other songs, such as *kra* rhyming with *frau, klupfe* with *tropfe,* and *gelauben* with *schaben.* No doubt all of these rhymed in the rural dialect spoken in Oswald's region. Very charming is the onomatopoetic refrain, in which the girl gives acoustic rather than intellectual expression to the emotions she feels in her heart whenever she sees her true love:

Frisch, frei, fro, frölich,
ju, jutz, jölich,
gail, gol, gölich, gogeleichen.
Hurtig, tum, tümbrisch,
knawss, bum, bümbrisch,
tentsch, krumb, rümblisch, rogeleichen.
So ist mein herz an allen smerz,
wen ich an sich meins lieben buolen gleichen.

The loyalty of another lovesick peasant girl is commemorated in a parodistic morning song beginning *Stand auff, Maredel.* Here, instead of the traditional watchman rousing the lovers, the peasant housewife is waking the girl and commanding her to dig up the turnips, build the fire, cook the food, wash the dishes, and so on. She suspects that the girl is still lying abed because her lover, the hired hand Chünzel, is with her; and Maredel does not deny the charge. The housewife then assigns her even more chores and warns her that her reputation is at stake; but the girl declares that work is murder and that she loves Chünzel above all else. All the woman's warnings and commands cannot separate Maredel from her lover, who causes all her joy. Oswald must have composed this song for a non-Tyrolian audience, because it has no words of strictly local currency. As in the song *Sag an, herz-lieb,* the two parts are sung simultaneously, thus making the dialogue lively but unintelligible.

Another rustic song, *Frölich so wil ich aber singen,* ridicules the ambitions of a peasant yokel who confesses his love to a socially superior woman. It is not clear whether she is really of noble birth (*adelicher art,* 79/14), as she claims, or merely of more prosperous peasant origin than he is. In any case, the humor lies in the incongruity between his boorish origins and the high-flown courtly terminology, taken straight from *hôhiu minne,* which he uses in courting her. It should be remembered that such parodies did not denigrate courtly love service, just as the parodies of the liturgy did not desecrate the divine service. The humor lay not in the language of courtly love, but only in the discrepancy between the subject and the situation. After flippantly encouraging her rustic suitor for a while, the haughty lady of this song dismisses him with disparaging references to his peasant diet and activities and tells him to go back to his work of plowing, greasing the wagon, and feeding the horses, like others of his breed. This song is a good example of rapid dialogue—almost stichomythia—in which the individual speeches are all of two lines. A happier ending is provided for a rustic song of leavetaking, in which Nickel and Elselein part with mutual assurances of eternal love. As in the previous song, the dialogue is expressed in single or double verses. This song, beginning *O herzen lieber Nickel mein,* is rustic only in that the two names suggest peasants.

Perhaps the most refreshing of all of Oswald's songs is an eclogue in which a shepherd lad breaks down the resistance of a coy shepherdess. The song, consisting of fifteen three-verse speeches and a three-verse narrative ending, begins as follows:

"Treib her, treib überher, du trautes Berbelein das mein, a
zu mir ruck mit den schäfflin dein. ca
Kom schier, mein schönes Berbelein." ca
"Ich merk, ich merk dich wol, aber ich entuon sein werlich nicht. b
Dein waide, die ist gar enwicht, db
mein haide stat in grüner phlicht." db

"Drive your sheep over here, you dear little Barbara mine, come over to me with your sheep. Come right away, my lovely little Barbara." "I hear you well, but I really won't do it. Your meadow is no good at all. My heath is very green."

Undaunted by her refusal, the lad assures her that the snow is already melting and the flowers sprouting in his meadow; but she answers that the birds are singing sweetly where she is. He continues to praise his spot until she finally acquiesces, but only after he promises to make no advances, she being determined not to give herself to anyone until she becomes a bride. He promises, but surely with reservations; and the two are united, as the narrator tells us in the closing verses, until *an laid schied sich ir baider wat* (v. 48). It is not clear what is meant by this last verse, which literally says, "Their clothing separated without sorrow," unless the word *wat* then had some other meaning unknown to us now. Since the shepherd calls his shepherdess Berbelein, or "Little Barbara," it is possible that Oswald was singing to Barbara Jäger, the reality behind the legendary "Sabina," whose name never once appears in any of Oswald's songs.

Far more rustic, and less idyllic, is a song beginning *Frölich geschrai so well wir machen,* which is difficult to interpret because it largely consists of rather transparent but otherwise unrecorded metaphors for sexual intercourse. The same technique of suggestion in place of exposition is used in *Ain graserin,* where a peasant lad tells how he has helped a goosegirl with her tasks. His actual words are innocent enough, for he merely says that he helped her repair her fence, cut the clover, and stack the grass; but in every case it is clear that he is really referring to erotic play. The humor of this song was certainly obvious to Oswald's audience; and we may be sure that his innocuous circumlocutions were already in common use.

Oswald's most successful use of transferred or metaphorical language is found in his song *Ain jetterin,* which Christoph

Petzsch has called Oswald's *Bergwaldpastourelle.* There is nothing rustic about the song, except that the girl is a country wench, presumably a berry picker or gatherer of mushrooms or some other forest produce.

I
At a wild height on a steep mountain a young, fresh, free, and frank berrypicker gives me joy and high spirits at the time the forests are putting forth their green leaves. Motionless I wait for her in quiet ambush just like a fox in a hedge. Look out from the bushes, Lynx, and keep low, creeping on all fours without causing fright, until I can snatch her snatch.
REFRAIN
Her red and genteel mouth is pure and sweet as sugar. Her feet are small, her legs white, and her breasts firm. Her words and gestures are rustic and charming.

II
I cause the blackbirds and many a select thrush much distress high up on the Lenebach with a trap that catches them when I jerk the string in a pleasantly green hut, well concealed with leafy branches. She who can arouse me with complete joy comes to comfort me, sneaking through the opening boldly yet furtively.
REFRAIN

III
When I discontinue my fowling and have secured all the gear, then you can still hear, to be sure, a sweet bird-call with much chatting for a short time. The fair one might well smile because she is stealing away all the art I have learned about fowling. Her trap *[kloben]* is too much for me—it demands the *gümpel* too often, and all that makes the hut creak.
REFRAIN

This is an amazingly skillfully and economically constructed song. The first strophe gives us a picture of the berry-picker and also reveals the fowler's amorous intentions, and the second explains how he traps birds. The third uses fowling terminology to relate the seduction; and in doing this Oswald has used unusual finesse in making the words meaningful on both levels. The word *kloben,* a cloven stick used for trapping birds, was commonly used as an obscene anatomical term, as was the *gümpel,* which literally meant "bullfinch" but was also used metaphorically to designate the male counterpart of the *kloben.* To appreciate the trick ending properly, we must understand the *gümpel* to be the victim of the trap, not the decoy as previous scholars have imagined. This song presents a favorite motif of medieval masculine humor, the insatiable seducée, or the seducer seduced. Also, the creaking of the hut suggests the popular motif of the creaking bed, which signifies the triumph of Eros. It will be noted that Oswald made metaphorical use of many fowling and trapping terms. For example, in alluding to the attempt on Sigismund's life in Perpignan, he states that to catch a bird one must lure and decoy it, for many a noble bird is deceived in nets, snares, and traps (19/17–24). The same image is used of women who snare men, for example in the song *Tröstlicher hort* when Oswald tells his lady that her trap and net have completely ensnared him (56/23/24), in *Gar wunniklich* when he tells her that he is held in the snare of her arms (64/3), in *Wenn ich betracht* when he calls a woman "an adorned snare" (*ain gezierte strick,* 3/38), and in *Zwar alte sünd bringt neues laid* when he laments that, even after Sabina's death, her trap still spoils his happiness on earth (36/7). Even God sets traps for people (1/72), as do death (23/11–12) and the devil in hell (95/30). False tongues are also called a snare (107/7).

Whereas Oswald's fowling song is evidently stylized and therefore not necessarily based on actual experience, his hunting song *Wolauff, gesell! wer jagen well* seems to express his personal feelings and impressions during or immediately after a hunt. The song consists almost entirely of shouts and commands to the hounds, and these give it an ebullient and spirited ring. It may seem surprising that Oswald is describing a *Heckenjagd,* a hunt in which the deer is chased into previously prepared nets; for such a manner of taking game was generally scorned by the nobility, who thought it more sporting to pursue the game until finally bringing it to bay. This unsportsmanlike sport can be justified by the terrain around Schöneck, Wolkenstein, Hauenstein, and the rest of the Wolkenstein residences, which was too precipitous for the open chase. A startled stag could all too quickly reach a steep and rocky slope inaccessible to mounted hunters. Consequently, the lowland nobility's prejudice against the *Heckenjagd* could not spread to South Tyrol.

Most of the hounds in Oswald's pack have names found in medieval allegories, such as *Lieb* (Love), *Trost* (Comfort), *Stät* (Constancy), *Will* (Will), *Harr* (Perseverance), and *Wunn* (Delight). As a result, some scholars have thought that this must be an allegory, even though they could not decipher it. It is more probable that these were the actual names of Oswald's hounds and that they had been suggested, directly or indirectly, by the names of personifications, or let us say "canifications," in canine love allegories like Hadamar von Laber's *Die Jagd (The Hunt).*

CHAPTER 2

The Middle Years

I *Constance and Perpignan*

AS previously mentioned, at the time that Sigismund was elected emperor, there were three emperors, since neither Wenzel nor Jobst would withdraw his claim. In like manner, there were three popes: Gregory XII, John XXIII, and Benedict XIII. Sigismund's first effort at reforming the empire was to compel Pope John to issue a bull on December 9, 1413, convoking a council which was to convene in the following year. This council, perhaps the greatest and most spectacular ever assembled in Christendom, was held in the episcopal city of Constance on the lake of that name. Pope John arrived there on October 28, 1414, and Sigismund on Christmas Day. Wolkenstein, as captain of the cloister at Brixen, arrived on February 4, 1415, with Bishop Ulrich, whom he served only until taking service with Sigismund as *Diener und Rat* (servant and counselor) on the sixteenth of that month.

From his vantage point behind the scenes, Oswald was able to witness the intrigues and the power play of the high dignitaries both secular and spiritual; and from him we might expect a factual report such as that written by Ulrich von Richental in his *Constance Chronicle* or by Thomas Prischuch in his historical song about the council.[1] But Oswald tells us nothing about politics. To be sure, he expresses his sorrow at the state of affairs—not at the decay and corruption of church and state—but at the high prices demanded for food, drink, and sex. Very enlightening is his lampoon against Überlingen, a little resort town across the lake from Constance, where the churchmen and statesmen went for recreation. This song, beginning *Wer machen well sein peutel ring,* says that anyone wishing to empty his purse should ask the way to Überlingen, where fourteen mushrooms cost fifteen shillings, while one egg costs sixteen hellers and two eggs cost thirty-two. There is little meat, Oswald continues, and greens are all the rage; yet the portions are small and laymen hunger. Mush is made with water, and roasts are sliced thin, while venison and fish are outlawed and no one dares eat them. The wine is as sweet as sloeberry drink and so abuses Oswald's throat that he has lost his beautiful voice and can only think of his Tyrolian vintages.

The wine in Überlingen gives joy just as the sack gives joy to the donkey; and its sharpness curdles Oswald's blood and puckers his lips. The host, who is very modest *(beschaiden)*, can cut *(schaiden)* your money from your purse by charging twelve pence per feather in your featherbed. If a cart came by, he would take off its wheels. The pork is from hogs fattened on chaff, there are plenty of fleas for passing the time, and the peasant bread is not appealing. To make matters worse, the maid in the inn is the counterimage of the courtly feminine ideal: her breasts hang like bats, her feet are as narrow as a shield, her legs are as slender as thick beech logs, her arms and hands are as white as crows, and she is generous with blows. Oswald cannot praise the dancing in Überlingen, and even the stove in the inn is surrounded by crying babies. These are but a few of Oswald's grievances, which are wittily presented with all sorts of clever wordplays and unexpected twists.

Oswald's disgust can be shared by those who were unfortunate enough to live in Norfolk or San Diego during World War II; but we should remember that he had never studied economics and knew little of the law of supply and demand. Today, unless he has a monopoly, a merchant is morally free to charge as much as the market will bear. If he charges too much, his customers can go elsewhere. Such an idea was anathema in the Middle Ages, when a Christian was expected to charge a just price for his wares, and it should be noted that the German word *billig*, which now means "cheap" when applied to prices, then meant "fair" or "just." Oswald was unaware of the fact that a host must charge more when the general inflation makes the wholesale price of food rise along with the cost of labor. Although most of Oswald's censure concerns the prices, he also ridicules the rusticity of the town, where people eat boorish food such as turnip greens and porridge.

Ulrich von Richental, the chronicler of the Council of Constance, claimed that prices were successfully controlled and kept reasonable; and he even left a detailed maximum price list for every conceivable good and service. Whereas Oswald charged that one egg cost sixteen hellers, Ulrich claims that they were always available for one heller apiece. Yet it is hard to trust Ulrich, a citizen of Constance, who was naturally on the defensive after hearing so many complaints from people like Oswald. Moreover, he played an important part in planning the logistics for the council at Constance, which was chosen over Kempten because, being a port on a large lake, it could easily draw provisions from a large area. To the credit of men like him, the city fathers of Constance broke with medieval monopolistic practice by permitting tradesmen and artisans from outside to open shop in the city for the duration of the council. Oswald's parodistic description of the housemaid is typical of the times, for he presents exactly the opposite of the stylized ideal of feminine beauty.

Constance is celebrated in a humorous song, *Der seines laids ergeczt well sein,* which appears in MS A but was omitted from MS B. This song, concerning Oswald's beard as he dances with the girls in a dance hall, has many witty inferences and innuendos, which remained obscure until Müller noticed that the word "beard" could be taken literally or understood to refer to Oswald's purse. Müller's astute observation made it abundantly clear that, when Oswald reports how the girls plucked the long hairs from his beard, he really meant that they took the large coins from his purse. It also proved that the *freulin zart* of Augsburg who are mentioned in *Wol auf, gesellen* (122/2) were not the prim and proper patrician girls envisaged by previous critics. Oswald's description of the boisterous dancing and fisticuffs must have greatly amused his fellow sufferers in Constance. In case the beard metaphor was not yet known, he could easily have revealed it by stroking his purse each time he called it his beard. Oswald did not compose new melodies for these last two songs but reused the one he had composed for *Mein buol laisst mir gesellschaft zwar;* and he omitted both from MS B. They were merely "occasional songs" to celebrate his adventures in Constance and Augsburg as entertainment for his companions, and he may have felt that they lost all significance when he shaved off his beard.

Although there is no clue as to its date of composition, scholars assume that Oswald's most famous drinking song, the one beginning *Wol auff, wir wellen slauffen,* was composed during his sojourn in Constance. This song depicts the conclusion of a jolly drinking bout, when the carousers are about to go home so that "no laymen, monks, or priests" will get to their wives before they do. But first they wish to empty their glasses so as not to part from such good wine, which they are determined to finish even though it paralyzes their legs. In going they must carry the prince *(fürsten)* gently so that he will not knock them down, for he has caused them much joy. The last strophe is enigmatic. It may merely ask whether the beds have been prepared by the housemaid, who has already oversalted both the kraut and the porridge; but there is probably some hidden erotic allusion. For unexplained reasons, it has been assumed that the prince who must be carried is Duke Frederick; but this is unlikely, since Oswald never enjoyed such cordial relations with him as he did with Sigismund, in whose employ he then was, or with Rhinegrave Ludwig, who was in secular command of Constance during the council. On the other hand, Burghart Wachinger has suggested that *fürsten* may have been the name of the wine they were drinking, an interpretation that would better explain its knocking them down *(fellen).*

Oswald found an early release from his annoyances at Constance on March 20, 1415, when Sigismund sent him on what was to be the most glamorous of his journeys, a voyage leading him to Portugal, North Africa, Aragon, Perpignan, Narbonne, Avignon, and Paris. Oswald commemorated this journey in a song of twenty-eight strophes beginning *Es ist ain altgesprochner rat.* This quixotic song tells us very few facts about the journey. Instead it presents only those highlights which Oswald particularly wished to remember and to recall to his audience, probably his cronies at Constance who had been with him in Perpignan or had at least heard much about what had transpired there.

Although this song tells us nothing about the route Oswald took to Perpignan, other songs indicate that he went to Lisbon, probably via England and possibly also via Scotland or Ireland. In Lisbon he joined King John's expedition against the Moorish stronghold Ceuta; and, if we trust another of his songs (26/12), he participated in its capture, which occurred on August 21. In view of the speed with which he returned from Ceuta to Perpignan, it has been surmised that he belonged to the embassy sent to announce the great victory. In this case, the reward he received from the queen of Aragon may have been a *botenbrôt,* the guerdon given to the bringer of good tidings. Unfortunately, Oswald tells us nothing about the early and most interesting part of his trip but puts us *in medias res* with Sigismund's gala reception in Perpignan, where he had gone in order to win over Pope Benedict's adherents. Benedict, or Peter de Luna as he was called in civil life, still commanded the allegiance of Scotland and the Iberian countries.

Before beginning his narration, Oswald cites an ancient proverb which states that no one can experience pleasure without experiencing sorrow as well; and then he adds that all the pleasure he had ever enjoyed had to be paid for in Catalonia and Spain, where people eat chestnuts. This absurd and irrelevant introduction sets the tone for the entire song, which is concerned only with trivialities. Next Oswald seems to say that the pain suffered by his beard and his purse in Constance was made good in Aragon and Perpignan, although this would contradict the tenor of his introductory statement. In any case, it is clear that this strophe would make sense only to those familiar with Oswald's "beard-songs" (to use Müller's felicitous term); and this is, accordingly, one of the many cases in which he alludes to his own songs. The next strophe is devoted to the proverbial saying that many a noble bird has been lured and caught in a trap; and this seems to apply to the following strophes, which refer to an attempt on Sigismund's life by saying that a hot bath was prepared for him (19/38).

What impressed Oswald most was not the attempted assassination, but the gala festivities with which Sigismund was entertained, particularly the long trains, earrings, and red fingernails worn by the ladies and their custom of welcoming visitors with a kiss. In addition, he noted that Sigismund liked this kind of greeting, especially from the young women. Had the schism existed between Sigismund's party and the ladies, it could have been reconciled much more quickly than with Peter Schreufel and his servant, the devil. Here Oswald has made a pun by using the German word *schreufel,* meaning a little screw, to render the name Luna, which, in Spanish, had that meaning, among others. Like a true child of his age, Oswald remembers with pleasure the pomp and ceremony, particularly the fanfares, the music, the costumes, and the lavish floats carried in the festive reception. When the negotiations failed, Sigismund became angry and left Perpignan on November 5 for Narbonne, from whence he continued to Avignon.

What Oswald remembered most fondly in Perpignan were the schoolboy pranks played by the high dignitaries in Sigismund's entourage. When Count Ludwig XII of Öttingen woke him up in the morning by rapping on his head like a raven pecking at a dead steer, he would answer by throwing a hobnailed boot in the count's face. Then he would get up, backside first, and wish Duke Ludwig of Brig a good morning by thrusting his bottom in the Duke's face, whereupon the latter would throw a shoe at him. But all this was nothing compared with the trick that Baumgartner played on Sir Fritz (Frederick of Hohenzollern),[2] namely, pouring a pot of stinking yellow "holy water" in his face while he slept.

After reverting for a moment to the attempt on the life of Sigismund, who defended himself like a man, Oswald suddenly shifts the scene to Narbonne, where the Concordat of Narbonne concluded on December 13 deprived Benedict of his last supporters. Oswald then describes the King's generosity and the general merriment occasioned in Avignon by the final solution of the Schism; and Oswald's full ridicule is heaped on Peterlein, the wicked cat, whose followers have now abandoned him. This time his pun relates the name Luna to the German word *Laune,* meaning "mood."

The crowning glory of this trip was the honor Oswald received from Queen Margaret of Aragon, who pierced his ears, inserted golden rings into them, and also fastened a diamond to his beard. On this occasion, Sigismund gave him the title of Viscount of Turkey and a fancy Moorish costume in which he could dance and sing like a pagan. Since Oswald was usually concerned only with his own person, we do not know whether the other celebrants were also in costume. In Paris, where the entire populace greeted the successful diplomats on March 1, 1416, Oswald stole the show with his antics. Next Sigismund and his retinue were honored by the students and faculty of the university; and then Oswald's beard received another diamond, this time from Queen Isabella of France, the Bavarian wife of Charles VI.

Oswald states that Sigismund rewarded him with as much gold as he and two helpers could carry. This sum, which we may assume to be exaggerated, probably included Oswald's annual salary of three hundred guilders, since his first year in imperial service was just ending. Oswald had to depart, apparently for Constance, because of an urgent matter; and Sigismund proceeded to England to reconcile the kings of England and France and thus end the Hundred Years' War. Oswald then praises Count Amadeus of Savoy, whom Sigismund had elevated to the rank of duke on February 20, on which occasion a grandstand crashed and injured many people, including Count Ludwig of Öttingen. It has been suggested that Sigismund's generosity toward Oswald was made possible by the money he received from Amadeus in return for bestowing the rank of duke. Being emperor was an honor, but a costly one, except on those rare occasions when he could recoup his losses.

This eccentric and confused medley of reminiscences ends on a philosophical note. Oswald concludes that, on the Day of Judgment, a clothes bag will be worth no more than a purse, and a belfry no more than a vinegar jug. He would have sung better if he had served his soul according to its need so that it would not be damned. Heinz Rupp believes that this ending is sincere and explains the intended triviality of the whole song, but one might also argue that the ending, like the prologue, was merely an adornment added in obedience to current fashions. In this case the real purpose of the song would be an attempt, on Oswald's part, to gain attention by entertaining his colleagues in Constance, who had seen and heard enough about power politics at Perpignan and preferred to hear of trivial and comic incidents, as is so often the case at reunions.

The climax of Oswald's journey to Perpignan was clearly the honor he received from the queen of Aragon, which he describes as follows:

Noch ist es als ain klainer tadel, a
seid mir die schöne Margarith b
stach durch die oren mit der nadel a
nach ires landes sitte. b
Dieselbe edle künigin, c
zwen guldin ring sloss si mir drin c
und ain in bart verhangen. d
Also hiess si mich prangen. (19/153–60) d

All this is no reproach, since the beautiful Margaret pierced my ears with a needle according to her country's customs. The same noble queen fastened two golden rings in them and hung one in my beard. Thus she had me adorned.

Even though Queen Isabella *(Elst von Frankereich)* also attached a diamond to his beard, Oswald seems to have been more gratified by the honor he received from Margaret. In any case, it is the only event of his first thirty-eight years that rated a complete episode in his farewell to youth, where it warrants the following eight verses:

> Ain künigin von Aragon was schon und zart,
> da für ich kniet zu willen, raicht ich ir den bart.
> Mit hendlein weiss bant si darein ain ringlin zart
> lieplich und sprach: "Non maiplus dis ligaides."
> Von iren handen ward ich in die oren mein
> gestochen durch mit ainem messin nädelein.
> Nach ir gewonheit sloss si mir zwen ring dorein.
> Die truog ich lang, und nennt man sie raicades. (18/33–40)

A queen of Aragon was beautiful and tender. At her request I knelt before her and held out my beard to her. With white little hands she sweetly fastened a lovely ring in it and said: "Never unfasten it." By her hands my ears were pierced with a brass needle. According to her custom, she fastened two rings in them. I wore them a long time, and people call them raicades.

Oswald says "a" queen instead of "the" queen, because there were then two ladies in Aragon with the social rank of queen, namely the young queen-widow, Margaret of Prades, and the somewhat older reigning queen, Eleanor of Albuquerque, the wife of King Ferdinand the Just, who was to die the following year. Whereas it was a Spanish custom to wear earrings, there is no evidence that it was customary to put rings in beards. Perhaps the queen had intended to attach the ring to Oswald's jerkin; but he, a born jokester immensely proud of his beard, may have thrust it out for the queen, who rose to the occasion and attached the ring to it. Because her words, as recorded by Oswald, do not conform to any known Iberian dialect, scholars assumed that he made them up, until Leo Spitzer proved that they represented a common language shared by several Iberian courts. This regal ceremony may very well have initiated Oswald into some order, perhaps the Order of the Griffin; for a later song implies that he received a *liberei,* or decoration, on his journey to Spain (26/8). His medallion is actually shown on the portrait that graces MS B.

II *Margaret von Schwangau*

After relating his various adventures, the thirty-eight-year-old Oswald concludes his farewell to youth by saying that he has sowed his wild oats long enough and thinks it time to hear his own child crying legitimately, which was a typically Oswaldian way of saying that it was time for him to settle down and have a legitimate child and heir. Nevertheless, he hesitated to marry, because he could neither forget the great love of his life nor hope to find her like. Besides, he was afraid of wifely scolding. His Perpignan song relates that he received a generous sum from Sigismund, perhaps not as great as he wittily claimed, yet possibly enough to finance a marriage. It may be significant that he compared this reward to the dowry given with a noble wife (19/151).

Whereas Oswald followed literary tradition in describing his marriage as guided by love, he had followed practical considerations in selecting Margaret von Schwangau, who brought him a generous dowry. Presumably the marriage, or one might say merger, occurred soon after Oswald's return from Perpignan to Constance, in other words, not long after he composed his famous farewell to youth. Whether he chose Margaret through love or expedience, it was a happy choice which he never regretted. As we shall see, their early life together seems to have been compatible; she bore him five children and stuck by him through thick and thin in all his self-caused misery. Her tender affection still shows in a letter she wrote to him only a few months before his death.[3]

Needless to say, Margaret inspired many of Oswald's songs, the first of which may have been a song of courtship beginning *Ain guot geboren edel man,* a *wechsel* (exchange), or a duet, in which the two voices sing alternate strophes. After a three-verse narrative introduction stating that the "wellborn nobleman" is courting a *freulein wolgetan* (lovely damsel) and is speaking to her with great propriety, the suitor begs her to grant him mercy.

She answers that he must be making fun of her and that, if he is really so badly off, he should ask God, not her, for help. When he insists that his lovesickness is truly critical, she assures him that she is not the girl he is looking for, that she is ugly and twenty-four years old, and that she can sing neither words nor melody. If she became his treasure today, he would regret it tomorrow. He answers her that she has captivated him and that he is much concerned about her honor. She thanks him for his concern yet insists that her reputation is not in danger. While appreciating the offer of his service, she considers him too high-brow for her. The girl states that she is twenty-four years of age. If the song, which seems to have been written in 1417, was actually addressed to Margaret, then Margaret would have been born about 1393, or some four years after Sabina.

Although Margaret denies that she can sing words or tunes, we may be sure that she herself performed the female role in this duet, no doubt after their marriage and for their friends; and the same is probably true of the duet *Von rechter lieb krafft,* which is unusually trite in content. In criticizing the superficiality of some of Oswald's lyrics, particularly those composed for polyphonic songs, we should remember that they were improvised primarily as vehicles for carrying the melody. No one would judge Mozart by his librettos, even if he had written them himself; and surely Wagner's verses are never held against him.

In the previously mentioned little song *Gar wunniklich,* Oswald again announces that Margaret has captivated and ensnared him and that he is her slave. When she asks him about his intentions and warns against the danger of slander, he pledges his loyalty and says that her sweet red mouth relieves him of his sorrows.

Very touching is a *Danklied* (song of thanks) which Oswald composed for Margaret when she accepted his proposal. Using the language of the minnesingers, he declares that now all his sorrow has been remedied by the knowledge that she has accepted him. In the second strophe he plays with the letters G, R, E, and TT, which are dear to him because they spell the affectionate name by which he calls her. In the third strophe he asks her to forgive any vexation he has caused her, and he again assures her of his concern for her good name and of his hope that they will not be parted until death and for a hundred thousand years thereafter. Oswald also plays with the letter *M,* for Margaret, in a tender little eulogy beginning *Rot, weiss, ain frölich angesicht;* and he calls her his *höchstes G* (Highest G) in a song of separation (97/21).

In another song written in this period Oswald calls his wife *Gredlein, Gret, mein Gredelein;* and she calls him *Öslin.* This marital hymn is a dialogue in which the parts consist mostly of three verses, although there are a few parts consisting of two verses, or even of one. Perfect marital harmony and fulfillment are suggested by the way in which the individual parts, having no rhymes of their own, are interwoven with common rhymes. For example:

Du kanst mich *nicht* erfreuen *bas,* ab
wann das ich *läg* an deinem *arm,* cd
verslossen als ain kleuss*ener*." e
"In deiner *phlicht* wurd ich nicht *lass,* ab
an sainlich *träg* mach ich dir *warm* cd
Und ist mir das ain klaine *swer.* (77/14) e

"You cannot make me happier than when I am lying in your arms shut in like a hermit." / "My love for you will never grow cold; without tiring I shall make you warm, and this will be a pleasant task."

Despite the frank sensuality expressed by both partners, this nuptial hymn expresses deep sympathy and sincerity.

Margaret's name appears both as Gret and Margaritha in *Do fraig amors,* a polyglot song composed of crumbs of German, Italian, French, Hungarian, Wendish, Flemish, and Latin, which has little to commend it except its novelty; and it also appears in two songs of matrimonial longing (33/35, 97/29), still to be discussed somewhat later. The name Gretel also appears in the previously mentioned song *Her wiert, uns dürstet* (70/7); but, since many other names appear in the song, the name Gretel may have been chosen at random and the song may well have been composed before Oswald met his wife. The name Grett also appears in a polyphonic New Year's greeting beginning *Mit günstlichem herzen,* in which the couple, no doubt still newly wed, exchange pledges of renewed love and admiration. As in the case of *Gar wunniklich,* if we look upon the individual parts of this duet as separate strophes, as Klein has edited them, we could say that all its verses are *Körner,* since each verse sung by one partner rhymes with the corresponding verse sung simultaneously by the other.

Whereas all the previous songs were socially acceptable, Oswald's basic nature could not be suppressed forever, not even by marriage, as is revealed by a little song beginning *Ich hör, sich manger freuen lat.* Like all the preceding love songs, and like a majority of Oswald's songs, this one has three strophes. In the first, the poet declares that he has banished all other highborn women from his heart now that he has met a red mouth from Swabia. In the second he tells us that this proud Swabian, in whom he can find no fault, is dearer to him than all the others with her beautifully formed eyes, nose, mouth, and chin, her throat on which the skin is red and white and clear, her little arms and hands, and her breasts, that are firm and painted pure white. But Oswald does not stop there. His third strophe tells us that she is small at the waist with a thick, firm, and rounded seat, two pleasantly warm thighs, perfect legs, slender feet, proper decorum, and irreproachable behavior. Such a frank revelation of a wife's physical charms would shock a fastidious audience today, even if mitigated by the praise of her laudable conduct. The same is true of Oswald's song *Gelück und hail,* a New Year's greeting presumably also addressed to Margaret. Following the usual sequence, it first praises her head, especially her colorful mouth, her red cheeks, her bright eyes, small ears, and curly golden hair. The next strophe praises first her nose, teeth, chin, throat, neck, and white breasts, then her long fingers and slender hands, her bright stomach, her perfect pudenda, her large firm buttocks, and her small feet. This song does not try to describe the loved one as an integrated personality, but rather lists the totality of her sensually desirable parts. The third strophe praises her social and moral virtues.

Marital intimacy also characterizes the previously mentioned summer-song *Wol auff, wol an!,* which depicts the joy of the dancers, birds, and plants on a May-day morning. Ösli and Gredli are taking their pleasure in their open-air bath, no doubt in large oaken tub such as was customarily used at the time; and, while Metzli fetches buckets of water, the newlyweds play their little *Liebesscherze.* "Wash my scalp, little lassie." "Rub me, laddie, around the navel. If you help me, perhaps I'll catch your little rat." The allusion to the little rat *(retzli)* would be obscene if the whole setting were not so fresh, frank, and marital. The song is both a nuptial hymn and a nature song, for Oswald presents himself and his wife as a part of nature. In the very next strophe he praises May for bringing joy to *Mensch, loub und gras, wolf, fuxs, den has* (man, leaves and grass, wolf, fox, and hare, 75/44).

Except for the *Natureingang* (opening nature scene) of the song *Nempt war der schönen plüede,* none of the putative songs to Sabina are primarily concerned with nature, whereas many of the *Margaretenlieder* are deeply imbued with it. For Oswald, Margaret was part of nature, in fact, nature's greatest achievement. Oswald only once mentions man as being made in God's own image and enjoying dominion over the animals (8/29–36); but he often includes man among the animals. As we shall see, he even refers to him as a *menschlich tier* (2/1), or *bête humaine,* and maintains that he is inferior to other animals, who stand by each other in time of need (10/76ff). Oswald was one of those men who, the more they see of people, the more they like animals. In a summer song composed some time after his trip to Spain, and probably early in his married life, he urges all of God's creatures to enjoy the May; and among these he lists leaves and grass, worms, birds, wild animals, ladies, and peasants (21/5–22).

The role played by nature is particularly conspicuous in a dance song *Ir alten weib,* which was probably composed while Oswald was courting his future wife. This invitation to welcome the May after winter's cold includes not only old and young women, but also the animals in their lairs, leaves, flowers, blossoms, grass, worms, birds, and wild beasts (21/1–8). Oswald calls upon the birds to lubricate their rough throats, and upon the animals to renew their furs. Young ladies should become lively, and the farmer should plow another furrow in order to be able to bake next winter. All creatures, both tame and wild, are yearning for offspring, while Oswald's horse is neighing and the donkey laughing.

Whereas Oswald was formerly praising courtly life at the expense of rusticity, such as he found in Überlingen, he now finds it inferior to rural pleasures such as hunting, chasing, falconing, stalking, shooting doves, and seeking mushrooms with a girl behind the bushes. His mind then jumps back to the pleasures he enjoyed in Spain and Catalonia, especially to the girls who covered their white legs with red stockings and their eyes with black mascara. Each of the three long strophes ends in an eighteen-verse refrainlike tail, which is designed more for rhythm than thought. The last of these runs as follows:

Da zissli müssli,	Clerli, Metzli,
füssli, fissli,	Elli, Ketzli,
henne klüssli,	tuont ain setzli,
kompt ins hüssli,	richt eur letzli,
werfen ain tüssli,	vach das retzli!
sussa süssli,	tula hetzli,
niena grüssli	trutza trätzli,
wel wir sicher han.	der uns freud vergan.

These words were regarded as completely meaningless until Conrad Lester observed that they were taken from a children's nursery rhyme, which, in turn, was a corrupted version of an obscene song probably derived from ancient fertility rites.

There are several reasons for believing that this song was composed in or near Constance soon after Oswald's return from Spain, and while he was courting Margaret. First, his memories of Spain are still fresher and more vivid than in any other song; and he is still wearing his beard, to which he alludes twice (21/38, 81). It seems to have been composed near the Rhine (*Reinstram*, 21/97), and the nursery rhyme he incorporated in it originated in an Alemannic region. The Swabian area around Constance would meet all these requirements, and Oswald's only protracted sojourn there occurred during the famous council. Assuming that the *dich* in v. 97 refers to a person rather than the Rhine, it may very well have referred to Margaret.

III *Married Life and Political Activity*

Although many of Oswald's post-Constance songs concern marital love and summer dancing, historical documents indicate that most of his time was consumed by more pressing matters. Soon after returning home to claim his patrimony, Oswald had joined the Tyrolian lords in a conspiracy against Duke Frederick, the Hapsburg prince who became duke of Tyrol in 1406. Like most of the territorial rulers of the time, Frederick was seeking to extend his authority over the higher nobility or "free lords," who had previously followed their own devices as nearly sovereign rulers. Fearing the Duke's encroachment on their ancient rights, the Tyrolian nobles organized an *Elephantenbund,* or Elephant League, in order to free themselves from the Duke and make themselves directly subordinate to the empire by becoming *reichsunmittelbar.* Because the empire was so poorly organized, being *reichsunmittelbar* was tantamount to being independent. A year later, in 1407, the league was expanded under the name *Falkenbund,* or Falcon League.

Emperor Sigismund naturally welcomed these aspirations and encouraged the rebellious lords to the best of his ability, since he himself had designs on Tyrol. As previously mentioned, Oswald had switched from the service of the bishop of Brixen to that of Sigismund shortly after reaching Constance; and it is probable that Sigismund employed him as an intermediary in dealing with the Tyrolian conspirators. Sigismund granted Oswald three hundred Hungarian guilders "for the useful services that he has often done, is doing, and shall continue to do" *(oft nützlich getan hat, tegelichen tut und furbass tun soll).* This was probably a standard formula used in connection with such appointments, since every German was, theoretically, a loyal subject of the emperor and therefore his faithful servant; but it could also imply that Oswald had already been serving Sigismund secretly. Be that as it may, it is certain that Sigismund used Oswald as a go-between in negotiating with the rebellious Tyrolian lords.

Duke Frederick had arrived at Constance as the bodyguard of Pope John XXIII. When the Council attempted to depose him, Pope John fled from Constance with Frederick's aid on March 20, 1415. That was a severe blow for Sigismund, who had determined to save Christendom by forcing all three popes to renounce their claims so that a more universally acceptable candidate might be elected. Because of Frederick's perfidy, the *Fürstengericht* (court of princes) lost no time in declaring him an outlaw and freeing all his vassals from their oaths of fealty, which they did on the next day. A year later, on March 30, 1416, while Sigismund was in Paris, Frederick escaped from Constance; and that is perhaps the cause of the *ehaft not,* or legal necessity, that caused Oswald to leave Paris so abruptly (19/201).[4] We know nothing definite about Oswald's actions but can assume that he hurried home to the league to help organize resistance against the outlawed Duke. Deserted by most of his followers, Frederick had returned home as a fugitive; and it seemed as if the nobles had at last succeeded in making themselves *reichsunmittelbar.*

Although officially outlawed, Frederick still enjoyed the allegiance of those Tyrolians, particularly the townsmen, who would rather serve a territorial lord than be plundered by unruly robber-barons; and he still had enough wealth to hire mercenaries. Because of his financial difficulties, Frederick's enemies derisively called him *Friedrich mit der leeren Tasche* (Frederick with the empty purse); yet he always managed to find resources when he needed them, even enough to roof the *Goldene Dachl,* his town house in Innsbruck, with tiles of gold.

Meanwhile, Sigismund changed his policy, partly because, as ruler of various lands, he saw how dangerous a precedent it would be to allow the discontented barons to depose their lawful liege-lord, and partly because he needed Frederick's assistance in combatting the Hussites, the rebellious followers of the Bohemian martyr. Receiving no help from Sigismund, the Tyrolian rebels found themselves driven back to their own properties and besieged by the Duke's forces. In March, 1418, the three Wolkenstein brothers were besieged in Greifenstein Castle, a stronghold of the Starkenbergers, the leaders of the conspiracy. Catching the besiegers napping, the garrison made a sudden sortie, destroyed their camp, and pursued the survivors. This feat of arms inspired the first truly martial song in German, which begins:

"Nu huss!" sprach der Michel von Wolkenstain.
"So hetzen wir!" sprach Oswalt von Wolkenstain,
"Za hürs!" sprach her Lienhart von Wolkenstain,
"si müessen alle fliehen von Greiffenstein geleich."

Do huob sich ain gestöber auss der glüet,
all nider in die köfel, das es alles blüet
Banzer und armbrost, darzu die eisenhüet,
die liessens uns zu letze; do wurd wir freudenreich.

Die handwerch und hütten und ander ir gezelt, a
das ward zu ainer aschen in dem obern veld. a
Ich hör, wer übel leihe, das sei ain böser gelt: a
also well wir bezalen, herzog Friderich. b

"Now charge!" said Michael von Wolkenstein. "Let's chase them!" said Oswald von Wolkenstein. "To horse!", said Sir Leonard von Wolkenstein, "they must all flee from Greifenstein at once."

Now a cloud of dust arose from the flames down on the monticule, so that it seemed to be in blossom. Finally they had to leave us their armor and crossbows, and their helmets too, and we were happy.

Their war machines and shelters and all their tents were burned to ashes on the upper field. I hear that anyone who lends evil will be repaid with evil. That's how we will pay you back, Duke Frederick.

After the first three strophes, the scene shifts as the besieged party pursues the besiegers to the canebrake in front of Rabenstein Castle, where they kill many more of them. Oswald then identifies the enemy, namely, peasant levies from Bozen, Ritten, Meran, Häfling, Mölten, Serten, and Senesien. We should remember, however, that he applied the word peasant *(Gepawren)* to all commoners, even to wealthy and patrician burghers. Not only the scene, but also the rhyme scheme, changes with the fourth strophe, from *aaab* to *aaaa*. This would suggest that the last four strophes were subsequently added to the initial three, which make a well-unified whole by themselves. The Wolkensteins' joy was short-lived, however; for their momentary success did not long delay Frederick's return to power.

Two documents prove that Oswald was in Hungary during the spring of 1419, where he, no doubt, had gone to procure aid, as well as to collect his salary, from his employer Sigismund. After returning to Tyrol and remaining there for a year, he seems to have joined Sigismund's long-promised but disastrous crusade against the Hussites in the summer of 1420. John Hus had agreed to argue his case at the Council of Constance only after receiving a safe conduct from the emperor, but he had been apprehended and burned anyway. Sigismund had tried to keep his word, which Pope John overruled with the argument that Hus, as a proved heretic, did not deserve such consideration, since Christians were not bound to keep oaths made to heretics. Enraged by such perfidy, Hus's adherents expelled the Germans from Prague and resisted the Emperor's attempts to subjugate them; in fact they carried the war to all neighboring parts of the Empire, and even as far as the Baltic. Since the Hussites were excommunicated, no mercy was shown to them; and, consequently, little mercy was shown *by* them as well. To make matters worse, their blind but brilliant leader, John Ziska, evolved new military tactics employing mobile artillery in the form of the famous *Wagenburg,* or wagon fortress, and completely bewildered the German knights, who were totally incapable of coping with such innovations.

Numerous crusades were proclaimed against the Hussites; but all of them came to naught through the apathy of the various territorial rulers, who preferred to use their troops against each other. As we have seen, Duke Frederick exploited the situation to use his own levies to crush his rebellious vassals rather than contribute them to Sigismund's campaigns against the Hussites.

When Sigismund's army was defeated at Mount Ziska in July, the citizens of Prague besieged the imperial garrison of Wischerad Castle, among whom were Henry of Slandersberg and a certain Wolkenstein. Since Oswald had associated with Slandersberg in the rebellion against Frederick, it it most probable that he was the Wolkenstein caught in the siege. Having reorganized and strengthened his forces following the defeat at Mount Ziska, Sigismund attempted to raise the siege but was defeated once more; and the garrison had to surrender, after having devoured the meat of seventy-two horses.

It may have been during this period that Oswald composed a long, but hardly inspired, appeal in which he called upon the German nobility to unite and crush the heretics. Oswald begins this song, *Ich hab gehört durch mangen grans,* with an obscure allusion to the proverb that Lippel would be a good goose if he had feathers with which to fly. He then complains that the eagles, falcons, hawks, sparrow hawks, and merlins have failed in their hunting and have been beaten by a coarse goose. Here, of course, he is alluding to the emperor, and to the dukes, counts, and free lords who were defeated by the geese, a term of ridicule given to the Hussites because the name Hus meant "goose" in Czech.

Oswald's harangue reminds the German knights that God has given them their beaks and claws to serve Him and that they should, therefore, moult their old feathers and attack the goose. Although this song has little artistic merit, it does display Oswald's uncommon ability to use language metaphorically—in this case to use the technical vocabulary of falconry in a transferred sense. Oswald not only exhorts the German knights but also reproaches Hus and warns him that the devil is keeping a warm spot in hell for him and all other followers of Wyclif, the English reformer who had furnished Hus with most of his heretical ideas. Whereas all other birds in the world remain in the station to which they are born, only the goose wishes to grow crooked talons with which to destroy other birds; but, when it swoops down at them, it also plunges into hell.

Oswald states that there was once a song to the effect that "the best bird I know of was a goose,"[5] but now, in Bohemia, it is the worst bird of all. This goose would be defeated if God would only withdraw the weapons He has turned against us because of our sins. Oswald calls upon all good Christians to implore the Prince to avert His anger, which is now being manifested through great signs in France, England, Catalonia, Lombardy, and Bohemia in the form of *influoss,* manslaughter, death, and heresy; and, in his own name, he calls upon Maria to intercede with her Son. It would be interesting to know whether *influoss* referred to any kind of influence from the stars, or whether Oswald was specifically referring to influenza, the most epidemic of the star-caused ailments. If the word *influoss* designated the bubonic plague, this would be further grounds for believing that the song was composed in 1420, a year in which the plague was exceptionally severe.

Imprisonment

In his much-quoted farewell to youth, Oswald had made the ominous prediction that he would never be able to forget the woman who had inspired him for so long (18/101). Sure enough, despite an ostensibly happy marriage, he never overcame his passion for his first love. Consequently, it was not long before she, or her kinsmen, took advantage of his obsession. In the fall of 1421 Sabina invited Oswald to a rendezvous, where he was ambushed, bound, and imprisoned in Vall and Forst Castles near Meran. We do not know whether Sabina instigated the conspiracy herself, as Oswald assumed, or whether she was the unwilling tool of her male relatives, who were justified in such an action because Oswald had refused to accept the verdict of the bishop of Brixen or submit their dispute to another arbiter. It is quite possible that Sabina acted out of malice and vindictiveness against her former lover and his wealthy bride. In any case, an allusion in one of Oswald's songs (59/21) suggests that Sabina invited him to join her in a pilgrimage, which was then a convenient way for lovers to meet, as one might infer from a reading of the *Canterbury Tales.*

Oswald's capture was a shattering experience: he was chagrined at having been duped and outraged by Sabina's treachery. He was confined under painful conditions and felt himself in imminent danger of death. The result was a number of heartrending songs combining disillusionment, reproach, fear of death, religious fervor, and self-commiseration. Seven of these songs, all set to the same melody and, therefore, having identical strophic structures, are the first songs transcribed in Manuscript B. Of these, four or possibly five date from the first captivity, and the last is definitely from the third captivity.

The first of these songs, *Ain anefangk,* was probably composed for November 25, the feastday of St. Catherine, whom Oswald asks to intercede for him before Christ. He thanks God for casting him into prison, where he can do penance in this world for having devoted himself more to worldly than to divine love; because God is now punishing him through the woman whom he has faithfully served for thirteen years. Fortunately for Oswald, love is so strong that it conquers all and can even compel God to show mercy to sinners. Had Oswald loved God as he should have, he would not now be bound by five shackles, one around each ankle, one on his left arm, one on his thumb, and one around his neck, this being the way his sweetheart now embraces him. In conclusion, Oswald expresses fear as to where his soul will go, and asks Mary's child to stand by him and cause his enemies to do penance here on earth; and he swears that he was never hostile *(gevër)* to the woman.

This song is ostensibly a prayer to God, but at the same time it is a diplomatic song, because it seems to be addressed also to Sabina, who is keeping Oswald in prison. Exonerating her as a mere instrument of divine dispensation, he reminds her that he has served her loyally for thirteen years, assures her that he has neither hated her nor been hostile to her, and prays to God to let her repent of the sin she has committed against him. In order to repent effectively, of course, she would have to free him. Nevertheless, even though there may have been a practical purpose in these songs, they are based on lyrical effusions of Oswald's immediate impressions and emotions. As an "outer-directed" man, Oswald had few inner resources on which to fall back. Dame Philosophy never came to console him in prison as she had once done for the more "inner-directed" Boethius. However, as in the case of Goethe's Tasso, his art was an outlet for his agony, and he too could have said *"Wenn der Mensch in seiner Qual verstummt, gab mir ein Gott zu sagen, was ich leide"* (When other men grow silent in their agony, a god granted me to tell what I suffer).

The next song in this series, *Wach, menschlich tier,* is an appeal to the human animal to awaken and fear the Lord, who has given him body and soul. The first two strophes are a hymn in praise of God, who harrowed hell and created the world and everything in it and who preserves all living things. In the third strophe Oswald implores God Almighty to make Sabina repent so that she will loosen his fetters; for he merely drives her away whenever he asks her to remove even one of them. Here again it is uncertain whether he was aiming his song at God or at Sabina, since the misery it expresses should have moved either of them to pity. For a modern reader, the pathos of the song is somewhat diminished by a suggestion of levity, or at least humor, when Oswald tells how sweetly Sabina sang while extorting his money. To be sure, this is sardonic gallows humor, which confirms the depths of his feelings; for elsewhere he tells us that she was demanding four thousand marks and Hauenstein Castle to boot (59/41). In those days, humor was not out of place in an otherwise religious song; because medieval men freely mingled the sacred with the profane, and God had not yet forgotten how to laugh.

The humorous factor is considerably greater in the next song, which is, however, no less serious because of it. Being out of physical danger, Oswald could now assuage his grief with irony, his chief defense against reality. Since he saw fit to use the same melody for seven of his songs, including some very long ones, it is appropriate to cite a random strophe as a sample.

Wenn ich betracht, a
strefflich bedenck den tag durch scharpfs gemüete, b
der creaturen underschaid, c
ir übel und ir güete, b
so vind ich ains in solchem klaid, c

des übel, guot niemt verbessren, bössren mag. d
Ich hab gedacht a
der slangen houbt, da von Johannes schreibet, e
wie in der werlt kain böser frucht f
sich auf der erden scheibet: e
vil schnöder ist unweiplich zucht, f
von ainer schönen, bösen frauen plag. d
Man zemet liephart, löwen wild, g
den püffel, das er zeucht; h
der ainem weib die haut abfildt, g
und si die tugent fleucht, h
noch künd man si nicht machen zam, i
ir üble gifft ist aller werlde gram. i

When I reflect all day and critically consider with sharp scrutiny the various characteristics of animals, their evil and their goodness, I find one of such a nature that no one can better or worsen its evil or goodness. I have thought of the head of the dragon of which St. John has written that no more wicked creature crawls on earth; yet much more contemptible is the unwomanly behavior of a beautiful but wicked woman. Man tames leopards and wild lions and trains the buffalo to pull; but, if a woman flees virtue, no man can tame her even if he flays her; for her evil poison is inimical to the whole world.

Here we find misogynistic views which had been expressed by Theophrastus, borrowed by St. Jerome, and handed down by generations of celibate clerical woman haters. But we should remember that Oswald is speaking only of wicked women. The next strophe tells how,

if such a woman is honored, she becomes overbearing with pride. If, on the other hand, she is spurned, she rages like the sea. If she becomes impoverished in rank or wealth, she at least remains rich in wickedness. A woman dishonored Paradise, because of which Adam was disgraced. Methuselah and mighty Samson were degraded and blinded by women; David and Solomon were treacherously betrayed by women. Aristotle, a great master, was overcome by a woman; he never profited from his knowledge, for she rode him at court.[6] King Alexander and beautiful Absalom both fell because of women. A beautiful but wicked woman is an adorned snare, a spear of the heart, a false friend who averts his eyes, a pleasure of deceptive sorrows. Because of that, Elijah was sent far away, and Joseph was chained deep in a dungeon. A holy man named John the Baptist was beheaded through a woman's vengeance, from which Christ may protect us. Also stultified *(betoubet)* and captured by a woman was von Wolkenstein, who limped many a step because of it. Therefore, I advise both young and old to flee the brilliance of wicked women. Think of their inner nature, for their sting is poisonous. And serve pure and virtuous women. I praise them above all jewels.

Here we find another favorite topos of medieval literature, that of the *Liebesnarr*, or dupe of love. Whereas most writers had named only three or four of these famous fools from the Bible and classical antiquity, Wolkenstein lists nearly all of them and adds himself as the last, but not the least, of their number. It is entirely possible that this clever twist was suggested by the roof of the well in the courtyard of the cloister at Neustift, which lies only a stone's throw from Brixen; for seven sides of the octagonal roof depict the Seven Wonders of the World, while the eighth depicts the cloister of Neustift.

The preceding two "diplomatic" songs must have been composed, or at least conceived, while Oswald was still imprisoned at Vall or Forst, since he was trying to appeal to Sabina's sense of pity, or at least to her sense of shame. The third, in contrast, must have originated after December 17, when Oswald was put into Duke Frederick's custody and was no longer at Sabina's mercy; for he was now free to say what he thought of wicked women and even to imply that Sabina was among the worst of them. There is another clue that some time had elapsed between his first incarceration and the composition of this song, namely, his statement that he has limped many a step (*des hanck er manchen tritt,* 3/48); for he could not have taken any steps while so tightly shackled. The second song, *Wach, menschlich tier!,* seems to have germinated while Oswald was still fettered, because he uses the present tense in praying for the woman at whose command his shin is being broken (*in der gebot man mir zerbricht die schin,* 2/42). The first song, *Ain anefangk,* seems to have originated while he was still in prison; yet he talks about his shackles in the past tense (1/98–108). This suggests that these songs, first outlined while Oswald was still in chains, were elaborated somewhat later, but soon enough for the original impressions to have remained vivid. It will be noted that all three songs have the same melody. This suggests that, deprived of his musical instruments and suffering physical pain and mental anguish, he was in no condition or mood to compose new melodies, whereas he was quite capable of giving vent to his frustrations in an already familiar melody.

It must have been near the end of his first captivity that Oswald composed the bitterest and most virulent and sarcastic of his songs, which showed that his love for Sabina had turned into outright hatred. The rhyme scheme of this song is a relatively simple one he often used: aaabcccbdddbeeeb. This enabled him to say what he really meant, even if he did speak metaphorically for the sake of irony. The first strophe, beginning *Solt ich von sorgen werden greis*, says that, if he is ever to grow gray from worry and become wise after suffering harm, it will come from the cuff-links his sweetheart has given him. She, at whose request he once secretly wore a golden chain on his arm, has now entirely forgotten it. Instead, she now lets him wear an iron ring three fingers wide; and he must look on while she makes up to a man who has done him much harm.

The second and third strophes continue in this vein. Oswald complains that Sabina betrayed his trust when he joined her on her pilgrimage; and he states that no saint would have held it against her if she had failed to make the pilgrimage. But, upon thinking the matter over, he has decided that she really did invite him for his own good. If she had brought him to heaven, he could have interceded for her there in return for having caused such a heavy leg-iron to rub his shinbone so lovingly. But all that can be averted by good spirits, since nothing love does can hurt. The dearer the child, the larger the stick; and she was once fond of him. Oswald could well see that, for she is steadfast; and rational love desires compensation. That is why he was so nicely hoisted by his feet to a beam. Her heart desired four thousand marks and Hauenstein, and it was all a big joke for her. Oswald could well see all that when the pain made him creak in his bonds. When Sabina piped the cat's tune, he squeaked the mouse's melody. For her sake five irons lovingly embraced him for a long time; and the whole matter spoiled his appetite. This song shows that Oswald no longer considered Sabina the divine instrument, but rather the human agent, of his suffering.

A humorous song, this time filled with irony and self-deprecation, seems to have been composed near the end of Oswald's first captivity, while the injury to his shinbone still made him limp. This song, *Es nahet gen der vasennacht,* celebrates *Fasching* (Mardi Gras), a period in which everyone should make merry. While all the others are paired off like amorous turtle doves, he is paired off with the crutch his sweetheart has provided to keep him company. The others may hug and kiss, but all he can do is to clutch his crutch. He ends the song by blaming his lady, who nodded to him so falsely in the autumn; and he damns her pilgrimage that has caused him to limp. It is not clear whether he composed this song in his cell, while hearing the merry sounds of *Fasching* from a distance, or whether the Duke let him attend the *Fasching* festivities, which occurred that year on February 24, for he was released less than a month later on March 18. That this song was composed in the spring of 1422 and, therefore, during the first captivity, is indicated by his saying that he was captured in the fall (*all gen dem herbst,* 60/30), which would logically mean "last fall."

The religious song *Hör, kristenhait,* which exhorts sinners to give up the world and live only for God, may also stem from Oswald's first captivity. This is probably true also of the otherworldly song *Ich spür ain tier,* which is generally attributed to the second captivity. Since the song is a memento mori, or remembrance of death, it would seem more suitable for his first captivity, while his life was truly on the scales (1/42). The remaining two songs to this melody would seem to stem from the second and third captivities and will, therefore, be discussed later. Several other religious songs have been ascribed to the first captivity, but without compelling reasons. Among these are four songs to the Virgin Mary: *In Frankereich, Wer ist, die da durchleuchtet, Gesegnet sei die frucht;* and *Wol auff, als das zu himel sei.* Since none of these makes any reference to imprisonment, they will be treated with Oswald's religious lyrics.

Although Frederick must have enjoyed seeing one of his rebellious subjects humiliated, he was theoretically impartial, and was acting only to see justice done to the Jägers. Consequently, to gain his freedom, Oswald had to promise to submit to arbitration and to demonstrate his good faith by depositing four thousand ducats (55/38). This large bail was paid by his brother Michael and three kinsmen, who then exploited the situation to exact even greater mortgages on Oswald's property and thus leave him financially ruined. In the past, scholars believed that Sabina became the Duke's mistress; but that charge is entirely unfounded, being based on a mistranslation of the verse *mit meines buolen freund muosst ich mich ainen* (26/112). This they understood to mean "I had to reconcile myself with my sweetheart's friend," taking "friend" in the sense of "paramour." The verse actually means that Oswald had to come to terms with Sabina's kinsmen, since they, not the Duke, were involved in the case.

On August 24, Oswald failed to appear for the trial despite the high bail; accordingly, the Duke arrested him in September and transported him to Innsbruck. Thereupon, Michael defied Frederick and joined his enemies; and Sigismund again intervened for his faithful servant Oswald by declaring Frederick an outlaw and proceeding to gather an Imperial army. However, because of the Hussites, Sigismund was still unable to proffer any real assistance; and the nobles' league submitted to Frederick in return for recognizing their privileges and declaring a general amnesty.

During his second imprisonment, Oswald was much better off than during the first. His brothers had made things so difficult for old Martin Jäger that he feared for his life and reduced his demands considerably; and on December 17, 1423, after more than a year of confinement, Oswald was at last released in the general amnesty without having made any major concessions. Oswald's second imprisonment seems to have allowed him much leisure for composing, provided he really composed all the religious songs that are generally ascribed to that period. In addition to the previously mentioned *Ich spür ain tier,* these songs include *Ich sich und hör, Du armer mensch, O welt, o welt, Wenn ich mein krank vernunft, O snöde werlt,* and *Kain freud mit klarem herzen.* None of these refers to imprisonment; but one of them, *O welt, o welt,* states that Oswald has lived in great joy for twelve and a half years. If this refers to his love for Sabina, it must have originated in 1422 and therefore very probably during the second captivity. Like several of the other songs so far mentioned, this one was a *de contemptu mundi,* or song denouncing the joys of the world. It resembles a palinode, a song denying everything the author has previously cherished; for Oswald denigrates not only wealth and honor but also foreign travel, composition and singing, and worldly wisdom. He concludes that all worldly joy must end in sorrow and that we must eventually part from all pleasure, wealth, and honors, since, as Everyman was to learn, nothing follows us in death but our good works.

Oswald used the same melody for another pessimistic piece, *Wenn ich mein krank vernunft,* which repeats many of the same ideas but with other words and images. Wealth and honor are not worth striving for, since the hour will come when we will gladly renounce them. Many a man thinks himself wise because he has learned to understand the course of the world, but he is really only a fool. As his authority for these statements, Oswald names Petrarch, whom he seems to have known only as the author of a memento mori. He who climbs highest will fall hardest, the poet exclaims, and it would have been better for him if he had been satisfied to remain halfway. Good turns into bad, but bad seldom turns into good. In seeking wealth and honor, people give up far greater treasures. Death is no respecter of persons, wealth and rank will not help; and king, emperor, duke, and count will all be Oswald's peers when they grin like apes. Wild animals live more in accord with God's commandments than men by desiring no more than they need and by helping each other in danger.

Oswald again praises animals as models for men in a song beginning *O snöde werlt;* and he avows that not even an ass would be a courtier, since a courtier must commit all sorts of violent deeds at his lord's command and spend all day currying his favor. Although this song is not dated, it must have been composed before Oswald submitted to Frederick and became a courtier, that is to say, while he was still maintaining his position as a free lord. If so, it was probably written during or between his captivities. Not only gold and silver are useless, but so are women's love, tournaments, jousting, running, dancing, and courtly pleasures. Oswald also uses the topos of *ubi sunt,* or "Where are they?," in asking where his friends, companions, parents, and ancestors are now, and where we will all be in a hundred years. He then marvels that he has not been able to separate himself from his lady *(meiner frauen),* who has betrayed him; and he says that his inexperience blinded him to the fact that she was a danger. One might assume that the "lady" is Sabina; but in this context it is more likely the world, which had been mentioned previously (11/110).

Another of Oswald's songs in remembrance of death, *Kain freud mit klarem herzen,* must have been composed during his second captivity. Because he says that he has wasted his days for forty-six years, he must have completed the song in 1423, most of which was taken by his second confinement. Again he expresses an extremely negative view toward life, which, in his view, not only distracts us from preparing for death but also brings us no joy. Like his other songs of *Weltabkehr,* or rejection of the world, this one suggests not a yearning for heaven, but only disgust for the world. Never, not for even a day, has he experienced joy great enough to overcome his hope, fear, and pain; and never has his joy in this world made him forget death's scythe. Instead of hope, he can feel only fear of hell's flames, which are inevitable for anyone who dies without confession, penance, and true remorse. Oswald concludes this lament with an invocation to Maria, whose Son can redeem us if we avoid that which displeases him.

All these songs of contempt for the world follow literary tradition. However, one of them, *Ich sich und hör,* alters tradition rather drastically; for, as Christoph Petzsch has observed, Oswald was prone to change and mix his genres.[7] To drive home their lesson about the meaninglessness of worldly life, clerical writers had often used the motif of the skull or skeleton that warns worldly people of the folly of their ways by showing them that all the worldly goods and accomplishments the owner enjoyed in his life cannot help him now that he is a stinking corpse and his soul is suffering in hell. Oswald has changed this image somewhat, making the speaker neither a corpse nor a skeleton, but a decrepit old man who describes his ugliness and physical infirmities. To be sure, the song has a frightening impact with its lurid description of pale color, red eyes, gray, falling hair, wrinkled face, faltering steps, heavy heart, bent posture, trembling lips, cracking voice, and decayed teeth, along with its warning to the handsome and erect youth that he, too, will some day be infirm with age; but somehow it does not actually teach a lesson or show that the horrors of old age are a punishment for a worldly youth. In the traditional form of this motif, the skull or skeleton can warn the youth that his soul's present punishment in hell is due to his failure to love God and do good works during his youth. Oswald's song might well persuade the youth to gather rosebuds while he may and make hay while the sun shines, since old age is bound to come no matter what we do, unless we die first. A similar lament for lost youth and complaint against the ravages of old age, but applied to an old woman, appeared later in Villon's *Les regrets de la belle heaulmière.*

His second captivity may have inspired two of Oswald's *Margaretenlieder,* namely two songs of forced separation. The first of these, *Senlich we mit langer zeit,*[8] is prim and proper, whereas the second, *Ain tunckle farb,* is somewhat less delicate.[9] The situation is the same in both instances: Oswald wakes up and reaches out for Gret, only to find that she is not lying beside him. In the first song, he laments her absence and curses the person who invented separation, with the imprecation that he might never enjoy another night of love with a beautiful woman. He then begs Gret to end his sorrow by joining him, as he is sure she will do because of her great steadfastness. The second song begins as follows:

Ain tunckle farb	von occident		ha
mich senlichen erschrecket,			b
seid ich ir darb	und lig ellend		ha
des nachtes ungedecket.			b
Die mir zu vleiss	mit ermlein weiss	und hendlein gleiss	ccc
kan freuntlich zu ir smucken,			d
die ist so lang,	das ich von pang	in meim gesang	eee
mein klag nicht mag verdrucken.			d
Von strecken	krecken mir all bain,		iif
wenn ich die lieb beseuffte,			g
die mir	mein gier	neur weckt allain,	jjf
darzuo meins vatters teuchte.			g

A dark color from the west awakens me with yearning, since I miss her and lie all night uncovered. She who can embrace me strongly and lovingly with her white arms and smooth hands is so far away that, in my fear, I cannot suppress my sorrow in my song. All my bones creak from stretching when I sigh for my love, who alone can arouse all my desires and the longing of my loins.

This song has been traditionally, but erroneously, classified as a dawn song, as morning songs are also called. Careful scrutiny will show that it lacks all the usual ingredients of this genre: it celebrates not the parting of lovers after a night of love, but rather their inability to come together. Consequently, it is not a *tageliet*, but rather an anti-*tageliet*, as Müller calls it.[10] Besides, the song may not even depict the dawn but the excessively long night. If the *tunckle farb* is interpreted as "darkness," then the darkness in the west could signify brightness in the east, which, in turn, would indicate the dawn. However, if it is interpreted to mean that there is color, even though very faint, in the west but not in the east, it would indicate the last faint reflections of the already set sun; and night would have already fallen. This would better suit the melancholy mood of the song. The scene would, then, span all night, from dusk to dawn. The second strophe continues as follows:

> Durch wincken wanck ich mich verker
> des nachtes ungeschlauffen.
> Gierlich gedanck mir nahent ferr
> mit unhilflichem waffen.
> Wenn ich mein hort an seinem ort nicht vind all dort,
> wie offt ich nach im greiffe,
> so ist neur, ach vil ungemach, feur in dem tach,
> als ob mich brenn der reiffe.
> Und winden, binden sunder sail
> tuot si mich dann gen tage.
> Ir mund all stund weckt mir die gail
> mit seniklicher klage.

All night I pitch and toss and roll restlessly. Yearning fancies approach me irresistibly from afar. Whenever I reach for my sweetheart and do not find her in her place, I suffer great distress, fire in the attic, as if the frost were burning. And then, toward day, she ties and binds me without ropes. Her mouth constantly arouses my desires with longing laments.

In this strophe, Oswald's vocabulary is rather ambiguous, for *gierlich* can mean either "longing" in general or "sensual" in particular. The image of fire in the attic would, however, suggest the latter, especially in view of Oswald's statement that Gret aroused the longing, not of his heart, but of his loins. The image of burning frost is an *adynaton*, or impossibility, a rhetorical device favored by Oswald. The next stanza continues:

Also vertreib ich, liebe Gret,
die nacht bis an den morgen.
Dein zarter leib mein herz durchget,
das sing ich unverborgen.
Kom, höchster schatz! Mich schreckt ain ratz mit grossem tratz,
davon ich dick erwachen,
die mir kain ruo lat spät noch fruo. Lieb, dorzuo tuo,
damit das bettlin krache!
Die freud ich geud auf hohem stuol,
wenn das mein herz bedencket,
das mich hoflích mein schöner buol
gen tag freuntlíchen schrencket.

Thus, dear Gret, I pass away the night until morning. Your dear form penetrates my heart, and I sing of it without concealment. Come, my dearest treasure. A rat is disturbing me with great defiance and causing me to wake often, and it gives me no rest early or late. My dear, cause the bed to creak. I feel supreme pleasure when my heart thinks that my beautiful love will embrace me toward morning.

Here again we find the ambiguous word *leib,* which sometimes means the whole person and sometimes only the body proper. In this case its primary meaning may be clarified by the word *ratz,* which has a hitherto unobserved secondary meaning.

On the surface level, the rat is a rodent constantly disturbing Oswald. This indicates that he must be in prison, since rats frequent prisons in literature as well as in real life. Nowhere else would he be disturbed by a rat constantly *(dick):* if he were a free man, he could take a cat or ferret to bed with him or move to another room. The prison setting would also explain not only why Margaret is absent, but also why Oswald has no substitute, as he certainly must have had when sleeping away from home. It would also explain why he is lying uncovered. If Oswald did compose his song in a dungeon, this might explain the dark color coming from the west, that being the only direction in which there was any window through which the time of day could be ascertained. In *Durch aubenteuer perg und tal* Oswald had specifically complained that, during his third captivity, he had been hidden from the light of the sun (*man barg mich vor der sunne schein,* 26/57).

But why would Oswald summon his dear wife to join him at the very time that a rat was disturbing his slumbers? Surely, she, like most women, detested such vermin. This suggests a secondary meaning of the word *ratz,* one evident in the previously mentioned song describing Ösli's and Gredli's outdoor bath. When Gredli promises to catch Ösli's *retzli* if he will first rub her navel, she is using the word as a metaphorical displacement for his male organ. This meaning is obvious in the song *Ir alten weib* (21/111), especially when Oswald's version is compared with parallel passages in *Neidhart Fuchs* and Fischart's *Geschichtsklitterung.* This secondary meaning of *ratze* may also explain an enigmatic passage in the Überlingen song, in which Oswald says he would exchange a *ratze* for a mallet helve (45/50). In Oswald's prison song of nocturnal longing, his sleep, which is haunted by sexual fantasies, is being disturbed by the same organ.

Despite our present "free speech" (dirty language) movements and general freedom in sexual matters, many readers will be shocked by such indecency in a song addressed to one's wife, especially one written to be sung in public and recorded for posterity; but fifteenth-century man was less squeamish in such matters, for *naturalia non sunt turpia* (natural things are not shameful). Nor would Gret, as a fifteenth-century woman, have felt degraded in being desired chiefly as a means of satisfying her husband's lust, the way emancipated heroines since Hebbel and Ibsen might well have been. This song was probably composed in Oswald's second and longest captivity, certainly not in his first when he was in excruciating pain and fear of death; for men in danger seldom think of love or sex.

IV *Political Journeys and Final Imprisonment*

After his second captivity, which ended on December 17, 1423, Oswald journeyed several times to Hungary to ask his friend and employer, Sigismund, to help him out of his difficulties with Frederick and the Jägers. These trips inspired several songs, which are somewhat obscure and have not yet been entirely explained. Perhaps the cleverest of these is the one beginning *Wes mich mein buol ie hat erfreut,* an ironic song in which Oswald blames Sabina not only for having lovingly suspended him by the feet, but also for causing him to go to Hungary, where he was devoured by seven-footed children, as he calls the fleas there. It might be well to mention that, whenever Oswald mentions Hungary, he is referring to a region now included in Slovakia.

Unable to enter the royal chambers in Pressburg (Bratislava) to present his petition to Sigismund, Oswald tricks the monarch into leaving his room by overstoking the fire in the tile oven through an opening from the corridor. Then, as Sigismund leaves the room in order to cool off, Oswald is able to confront him. As we shall see later, this version of the song was somewhat embroidered by the time it was recorded in MS B. This confrontation may have caused Sigismund to write his letter of December 15, 1424, promising to intercede with Frederick on Oswald's behalf. We know that Oswald had already been in Hungary on April 1, 1419, at which time he was provided with a safe-conduct; but it is most likely that the song was composed in 1424, when Oswald's situation was more serious. In any case, it was composed after the poet's first captivity, as we can see from Sigismund's sarcastic reference to Sabina as the cause of Oswald's woes (55/27–29).

In another song, beginning *Kain ellend tet mir nie so and,* we learn that Oswald's worst grievance in Hungary was that the inns were always full of children; for he was not temperamentally adapted to being a baby sitter. The crying babies were most obnoxious in winter when, after riding all day in the cold, he could find warmth only in the heated room, which was full of cradles. The babies' discordant crying prevented him from singing; and this denial was, of course, a great hardship for Oswald. In Pressburg he was once annoyed by a two-and-a-half-year-old child who, together with the lice, kept him awake all night. Whenever the child cried that it was thirsty, people brought it mead and wine as if it were a prince, as well as fish, foul, sausages, and anything else its heart desired. But even then it would not stop crying, until Oswald secretly pinched its little hide. This set Oswald to wondering how anyone could rear a child without thrashing it; and he reminds mothers that "the dearer the child, the bigger the switch" *(ie lieber kind, ie grösser besen),* which was his version of the adage about sparing the rod and spoiling the child. If parents give in to the child's will now, he postulates, they will be paid with much embarrassment later.

The song *Wie vil ich sing und tichte*, which will be discussed later, tells how Oswald nearly drowned on one of his Hungarian journeys by falling into a rocky stream. This accident seems to have occurred in 1424, because Oswald tells us (23/97) that it was two and a half years before his arrest at Wasserburg, which we know took place in the spring of 1427. The circumstances are, however, doubtful. Oswald never had a kind word for Hungary, which, for him, was a land where people used saddles for pillows (55/43).

Sometime between his second and third captivities, Oswald composed an unusual song lamenting the boredom he suffered during an involuntary residence at Hauenstein Castle. This song, which begins *Durch Barbarei, Arabia,* is sometimes known as the "Hauenstein Song," for Oswald is grumbling about his tedious life in that remote fortress. To emphasize his present isolation, he begins with an extensive—almost exhaustive—list of the countries he has previously visited: to wit, Barbary, Arabia, Armenia, Persia, Tartary, Syria, Byzantium, Turkey, Georgia, Russia, Prussia, Estonia, Lithuania, Livonia, the Nähringer Haff, Denmark, Sweden, Brabant, Flanders, France, England, Scotland, Aragon, Castile, Granada, Navarre, Portugal, Spain as far as Finisterre, Provence, Marseilles, and at last Ratzes at the foot of Schlern Mountain, where Hauenstein Castle stood on a narrow chimney-like *kofel,* or peak, jutting out from a steep mountain slope. This list includes some two thirds of the countries Oswald claims to have visited, the omissions being Apulia (12/4), Bohemia (12/3), Catalonia (19/7), Crete (18/15), Cyprus (12/5), Egypt (*Soldans kron,* 12/6; *Soldans lant,* 21/92), Picardy (21/95), Sicily (12/5), and Tuscany (21/96). By thus contrasting his previous glory with his present misery, Oswald was presenting himself as a truly tragic figure according to the medieval definition of tragedy, which was man's fall from high estate.

Despite all the effort Oswald had made, and all the danger he had incurred, in obtaining Hauenstein, he found no happiness there. The first strophe ends with a self-pitying complaint, which seems to parody a May song. The poet grieves at being restricted to a narrow round hillock surrounded by thick forests, where all he can see, day after day, are innumerable high mountains, deep valleys, stones, shrubs, tree trunks, and snow fences. A nineteenth-century Romanticist would have reveled in such an idyllic spot: Eichendorff would surely have praised God for the privilege of escaping to such sylvan solitude where he might contemplate His handiwork at such leisure. But not Oswald, or any other man of his age. Except for a few exceptional artists such as Albrecht Altdorfer and Pieter Breughel the Elder, Europeans hardly discovered the beauty of wild nature until the eighteenth-century Swiss poet Albrecht Haller celebrated rugged mountains in his poem *Die Alpen.*

Courtly poets liked well-cultivated gardens. At best they might approve the park landscape surrounding the castle as a setting for May dances and hunts; but the true wildwood was avoided as a weird and uncanny place to be crossed only under compulsion, as we see in the case of Beowulf seeking Grendel's mere or Gawain seeking the Green Knight's chapel. No medieval poet could have comprehended that a windswept crag or a snow-covered summit might be beautiful. Until the invention of snow plows, skis, and ski lifts, heavy snow on the mountains suggested hardship, isolation, and danger, rather than pleasure. Oswald's confinement was particularly painful, because he had to share the narrow *kofel* with his children, whose crying assaulted his ears. As he mentions in his farewell to youth, he had married in order to hear his own child crying legitimately; and in this he was successful, for Margaret soon supplied him with five legitimately crying heirs.

The second strophe contrasts the honors Oswald had previously received from princes and queens with his present social stagnation. Also, there is no red mouth to comfort him; and he can see nothing but goats, bucks, cattle, and coarse, black, ugly people who raise one's spirits like sour wine and lice. In his anxiety, he often strikes his children on their bottoms, whereupon their mother comes running up and scolds and strikes him. Now poor Margaret is no longer the ideal ladylove whose red mouth can cure him of his sorrows. She is the scolding wife, the termagant in the proverbial *Ehekrieg,* or matrimonial war. Oswald's fear of a nagging wife, which he mentions in his farewell to youth as a reason for not marrying (18/104), was already realized; but let us hope with Müller that this was only a literary stylization. Previous scholars, possessing little humor and less understanding of medieval literature, had assumed that the differences between Margaret and this shrew were so great that Oswald must have married again after Margaret's death. But that was before documents came to light proving that Margaret survived Oswald by some years.

Oswald's self-commiseration continues into the third strophe, where he complains that his only entertainment is the singing of donkeys and peacocks and the rushing of the brook, which nearly burst his head. Ugly rumors arrive that his territorial lord, Frederick, is angry with him; but this is due to wicked people. All his kinsmen hate him, but, of course, through no fault of his own. In conclusion, he requests good and virtuous people, especially the high princes, not to let the wolves devour poor Wolkenstein. Thus this complaint can be classified as one of Oswald's diplomatic or petitional songs. When Oswald calls himself "poor Wolkenstein," he is probably making a word play by using *arm* in the sense of both miserable and impoverished.

Oswald's feud with the Jägers was not only disastrous for the latter, but also annoying for Duke Frederick, whose duty it was to maintain the peace in his realm. Consequently, he once more summoned Oswald to attend a trial on March 16, 1427, at Bozen in order to settle the Hauenstein affair once and for all. But Oswald, whose delaying tactics were proving successful, preferred to miss the trial and take another journey. According to the opening of his song *Durch aubenteuer perg und tal,* he was setting out in search of adventure so as not to *verligen,* that is, to commit the unknightly sin of sloth. To avoid such indolence, he was making a sentimental journey to revisit all the scenes of his glorious trip, a decade earlier, to England, Scotland, Ireland, Portugal, North Africa and Spain. It is more likely that he really wished to miss the trial at Bozen and perhaps to make a diplomatic journey. In any case, Frederick, who was not napping, apprehended Oswald at Wasserburg on Lake Constance.

From Wasserburg Oswald was taken, tightly bound on his horse, to Vellenberg, where he was chained with two heavy fetters, "two spurs of chivalry" as he ironically called them. His only satisfaction seems to have been the unusual precautions Frederick took and the warning he gave his jailers not to take any chances with such an important prisoner. From Vellenberg the captive was transferred to Innsbruck with such a large guard that he likened it to a Prussian crusade *(Preussen vart);* and, still protesting his innocence, he could not see why he was so tightly bound and closely guarded; for, after all, he had not stolen the Imperial treasures. For the next twenty days he "was hidden from the sun"; and what he lost by tearing the knees of his stockings he saved by sparing the soles of his shoes.

Strophes 7–10 of this song help explain Oswald's purpose in mentioning his earlier journey to Portugal and Spain, it being to contrast his previous glory with his present degradation. Now, in place of royal personages, he has to consort with miserable, filthy jailbirds who pollute the very air; and in strophe 9 he expressly contrasts his recent dinner at Rhinegrave Ludwig's table with his present meals shared with such rabble. He also remembers having dined with the "Roman King," who has now forgotten him. His table-mates are an old Swabian named Planck, Peter Haizer and his wife, a drunken scribe, and a loud snorer named Kopp. His social pride reveals itself when he likens himself to a falcon in the company of calves. His disgust is so great that, for the only time in his entire oeuvre, he indulges in a kind of humor practiced to excess by most of his contemporaries, namely, jokes about breaking wind. But, even in this case, Oswald uses very clever and rather abstruse images involving a bass horn and the explosion of an overloaded cannon.

Luckily for Oswald, his friends among the Tyrolian nobility had not forgotten him; and the Kreigers, Greiseneggers, and other important counts and free lords interceded on his behalf. Because of their insistence, Frederick decided that it was better to have Oswald as a friend than as a foe, for "such people don't grow on trees" (*ja werden solcher leut von bomen nicht geboren,* 26/110). A true artist at heart, Oswald explained that Frederick freed him in order to hear him sing of beautiful ladies. Frederick's chancellor drew up an agreement with the Jägers; and Oswald was freed on May 1, 1427. He declares that his children will have occasion to wring their hands whenever they hear of the Hausman woman. In MS A this song has an additional strophe, omitted in MS B, which tells how the newly liberated Oswald successfully intercedes on behalf of a prison mate who had already served for eight and a half years. This, too, is a diplomatic song. Oswald asserts that, even though he has rebelled against his prince (26/89–90), the Roman King has completely forgotten him (26/86). Thus he can justify his sudden shift of loyalty from Sigismund to Frederick, whom he now flatters with the epithets "powerful, illustrious, and highborn" (26/106).

As so often, Oswald ends this lengthy song with a pious contemplation, namely, that he has deserved his punishment, which will cost many a farthing. He has deserved it, of course, from God, not from man; because he always considered himself entirely innocent in all transactions with men. The Hauenstein song states that his territorial lord is angry with him only because of the jealousy of wicked people (44/74), and in the present song, too, he considers himself entirely innocent (26/44). Since God is absolute, Oswald could admit his guilt toward Him, while remaining too proud ever to admit being wrong in this world. This is apparent in his song *Loblicher got* (7/49):

> Gen diser werlt hab ich die angst
> verschuldet sicher klain.
> Neur um den Got, der mir vor langst
> beschuoff von Wolkenstein.

I have little deserved this anxiety from the world, but only from God, who long ago created me, Wolkenstein.

Perhaps it is significant that Oswald never utilizes the traditional *Demutsformel,* or formula of humility, by which medieval authors were expected to assure their public that they considered themselves quite unworthy and incapable of performing as well as they should. Thoroughly assured of his skill, Oswald could not feign such modesty; instead, he frankly called himself a nightingale (*Seid ich nu haiss die nachtigall,* 81/26).

Although Oswald claimed that the reconciliation had cost him many a farthing, he actually lost very little in submitting to arbitration. His intransigence had paid off well, and he ended up retaining all of Hauenstein after agreeing to a nominal payment of 500 ducats to the Jägers, which was completed long after his death. Thus, after twenty years of feuding and litigation, Hauenstein remained in the hands of Oswald and his descendants. Equally important for Oswald was his final realization that he could no longer oppose his duke. Like his two brothers before him, who had made peace with Frederick in 1426, he at last saw that the old order was changing and that the lords of Tyrol would have to submit to the jurisdiction of their territorial ruler. For the rest of his life, he remained a faithful subject, one of those courtiers of whom he had spoken so disparagingly in his song *O snöde werlt* as having to curry favor with their masters.

It was probably at the end of 1427 that Oswald undertook a memorable journey to Heidelberg and Cologne, although there are also cogent arguments for accepting the older view that the journey was made at the end of 1423. In any case, it is celebrated in a very elaborate song beginning *Von Wolkenstein.* This travelogue relates Oswald's journey via Salzburg, Munich, Augsburg, Ulm, Heidelberg, and Cologne to Fürstenberg and back to Heidelberg, where he seems to have sung his song in honor of his host, Rhinegrave Ludwig. The strophic form is the same as that of his farewell to youth; but Oswald seems to have taken more pains with the meter and the rhymes, and he has composed a more elaborate melody. Thus we see that he was trying to show fitting respect to, and appreciation for, his highborn host.

In Salzburg, Oswald was entertained by a gentleman named Braun, to whose beautiful, virtuous, and courteous wife he wished many happy years; and this suggests that he might have been there on New Year's Day. Hearing of his arrival, Archbishop Eberhard III invited him to dinner. From Salzburg, Oswald was accompanied to Munich, where the knights and ladies entertained him; and in Augsburg and Ulm he was generously treated with wine. In the latter city he was invited to a dance, at which his feelings were hurt when he overheard a lady tell her husband that she did not wish to welcome such a beggar. Oswald seems to have thought that she was offended not only by his plain *(schlecht)* clothing, but also by his empty eyesocket; and he drew the conclusion that a person is unwise to judge by appearances. Since Oswald was, by nature, extremely vain and always a dandy, we may assume that his wardrobe had suffered from his recent imprisonment and his desperate financial straits.

In Heidelberg, Oswald encountered, in addition to Rhinegrave Ludwig, four prince electors: the archbishops of Cologne, Mainz, and Trier, and the Margrave of Brandenburg, Frederick of Hohenzollern, probably the same "Sir Fritz" who had shared quarters with him in Perpignan and had been doused with yellow "holy water." [11] These prince electors, together with representatives of the prince elector of Saxony and of various imperial cities, had met in Heidelberg to discuss the recent tax levied to support a crusade against the Hussites. At the castle in Heidelberg, Oswald was admitted into the count's chamber, where he seems to have spent the night. The next morning, at the Rhinegrave's expense, he was completely dressed up like a doll in a coat and hat of fox and marten, which was a big improvement over the traveling clothes that had offended the fastidious lady in Augsburg.

Oswald continued his way to Cologne by horse and ship, and from there to Aachen (Aix-la-Chapelle) in a noisy and bumpy wagon. Archbishop Dietrich of Cologne and Duke Adolf of Jülich and Berg received him most graciously and fulfilled all his requests; but Oswald does not reveal what happened next. After a pleasant return journey spent in testing the famous Rhineland vintages, he arrived in Heidelberg, where he was again royally entertained by Ludwig.

Although this is ostensibly a *Fürstenlob,* or song praising a prince, it is actually a political song. To be sure, Oswald does not betray his secret; but it is evident now, and probably was to Oswald's contemporaries too, that he had journeyed to Cologne and Aachen to be admitted into the *Femegericht,* the underground court of justice from which our Ku Klux Klan was derived.[12] By becoming a *Freischöffe* (magistrate) of that legal organization, Oswald was in a much better position to litigate against his enemies. Oswald traveled to Cologne because the Archbishop was the head of the entire *Feme* in Westphalia, its ancient homeland; and it is probable that, after receiving his endorsement, Oswald proceeded to Westphalia to be admitted into the secret order. Oswald tells us nothing about such matters, since all the doings of the *Feme* were top secret; but he hints that he is reporting nothing that transpired after his visit to Cologne (41/57).

If, as seems almost certain, this journey occurred in 1428, Oswald would not have needed the *Feme*'s support against the Jägers or Frederick, with whom he was now reconciled. Instead, he probably needed it against the Bishop of Brixen, with whom he was still feuding. The successful journey of 1428 was probably a realization of the one planned for 1427 but frustrated by Frederick at Wasserburg. This time Oswald must have had the duke's blessing, since one of the terms of his liberation had been that he would not leave Tyrol without the duke's permission.

On this journey, Oswald composed another song, *O phalzgraf Ludeweig,* a *Fürstenlob* in honor of Ludwig, who, as Count of the Rhenish Palatinate *(Rheinfalz),* was called *Pfalzgraf* as well as *Rheingraf.* The musical accompaniment to this song is most elaborate, and the words serve little purpose except to furnish the sounds to be sung. The rhyme scheme is exceptionally intricate.

O phalzgraf Ludeweig	a
bei Rein so vein, dein steig	hha
geit braite, schraitte tugent gross,	iib
Kainer dein genoss	b
dir nicht geleichen mag.	c
Hör mích, was ích dir sag!	jjc
Sich klärlich, bärlich vindet das	kkd
nach adelicher mass.	d
Die rüerstu, füerstu in stetem schilt	lle
durch manháit, weissháit warhafft milt,	mme
Ouch freuen dich die frauen, permafoi	gf
hort ich von deim getrauen	g
gemaheln von Sophoi.	f

Oh Palsgrave Ludwig on the Rhine so fine, your way is the broad way of great virtue. None of your peers can equal you. Listen to what I say. That is clear and most apparent, judged by the noble standards you meet and bear on your steadfast shield for the sake of manhood, wisdom, and true largesse. And you enjoy the ladies, by my faith, as I heard from your loyal consort from Savoy.

Obviously, the words are rather banal and serve chiefly to furnish the rhymes. The reference to Ludwig's shield, which would surely clarify the pertinent verse, suggests that this is Oswald's only venture into *Wappendichtung,* or heraldic verse, a form of flattery then practiced mostly by professional poets in the service of high lords. It seems inconsistent for a single strophe to combine such abject flattery with such intimacy. The second strophe praises Heidelberg, not for its romantic setting or its lordly castle, but only because of the red mouths of the Rhinegrave's daughters, who are referred to by the local diminutive forms of their names. The third strophe praises Ludwig's various territories or, more precisely, those famous for their wines; and it ends with thanks for the furs that Ludwig has given to Oswald.

CHAPTER 3

Later Life

I *Life at Hauenstein and Imperial Service*

After his final reconciliation with Frederick, Oswald's life became somewhat less tumultuous and allowed him more time for contemplation. A short time after his third imprisonment, he interpolated an additional strophe into a contemplative song he had previously composed. This song, *Wie vil ich sing und tichte,* is an autobiographical memento mori, in which Oswald recollects his seven most nearly fatal adventures as evidence that death is never far away. Only one of these narrow escapes had been mentioned in his farewell to youth, namely, his shipwreck in the Black Sea. A few weeks before this shipwreck, while jousting, Oswald had charged on horseback down a staircase into a cellar, where his horse broke its neck and he landed in a barrel of wine. Despite his predicament, he had the presence of mind to offer a drink to those who rushed to help him. The account of his next adventure is somewhat obscure, but it seems to allude to the fight he had with his brother Michael when he tried to steal his jewels and lay the blame on Michael's wife. But it may also allude to an ambush he once suffered during an amorous intrigue.

On another occasion, Oswald wished to learn to swim in the ocean; but he sank to the bottom and remained there for more than an hour(!) seeking fish with his nose. The next adventure was his capture by Sabina, who is described as a continuing danger to him. The Hungarian journeys forced upon him by Sabina caused the next peril, which seems to have been a plunge into a rushing stream. The seventh and last danger was his capture by Frederick, who intercepted him on his alleged trip to Portugal, Granada, Spain, and North Africa. That this strophe is a later interpolation is indicated by a reference to Sabina's recent death (23/120), for this event, which is not documented, occurred during the summer of 1425. Sabina was already dead when Oswald mentioned her name for the only time in his poetry, namely as *die Hausmanin* in the previously mentioned *Durch aubenteuer perg und tal.* Oswald seems to be sincere in asking God to forgive her for all the good and harm she has done him (*was si mir lieb, laid hat getan, das well ir got vergeben,* 36/12). Although the opening and closing strophes of the song *Wie vil ich sing und tichte* express fear of sudden death and Judgment Day, the song is unconvincing because of Oswald's levity in relating his skirmishes with death. It certainly fails to achieve the emotional intensity of his prison songs like *Ich spür ain tier.*

Another song is generally attributed to the year 1427, but without compelling reasons. This song, *Ain burger und ain hofman,* is written to the same melody as the memento mori *Kain freud mit klarem herzen,* yet it is altogether worldly in outlook, being a satire on human foibles. It follows in the popular tradition of *disputatio,* a genre often used for deciding or elucidating religious, moral, legal, or amorous questions. The song concerns a debate between a courtier, obviously representing Oswald, and a burgher, no doubt representing Hans Hausman, the rich old husband of Sabina Jäger. The two men are arguing as to who can better please the ladies, each claiming that he has greater amorous appeal; and they call upon an old procuress to act as umpire. The noble youth describes his beauty and ability to sing and dance, whereas the old townsman can only boast of his full purse. When the two litigants have finished pleading their cases in alternating speeches, usually of eight verses, the superannuated prostitute finds the burgher's money more attractive than the young knight's many accomplishments on the jousting field and dance floor; and she gives the victory to the older man. In anger, the youth strikes her and knocks out eleven of her teeth, whereupon the burgher compensates her for the injury by giving her five silver pounds and also a cow and a calf so that she will always have mush to eat, since she can no longer chew. He also promises to give her sausages and rolls if she will procure him a pretty girl who lives on the corner.

The old procuress in this song has done her pandering in Brixen, a fact which not only lampoons the clergymen of that ecclesiastical city but also suggests that the song was composed while Oswald was resident there as captain of the cloister. In this case, it may have been composed sometime before his sojourn at Constance, while he still felt resentful that a young noblewoman like Sabina could sell herself to a commoner, especially an aged one. It is also significant that Hans Hausman was a citizen of Brixen. Although this song was set to the same melody as *Kain freud mit klarem herzen,* it differs from it in being followed by a short strophe of eight verses, in which Oswald concludes that old women and ducks belong in a lake since no creatures quack more. The addition of a shorter strophe, or *tornade,* followed French tradition.

Another farcical poem, *Sich manger freut,* is usually attributed to this period of Oswald's life, but likewise without convincing reasons. As in many of Oswald's narratives, the episodes do not follow an exact chronological, or even logical, order; for he summarizes the adventure in the first two strophes before beginning afresh in the third. The plot is as follows: One day the narrator, calling himself Hanns Maler, quarrels with his wife for no good reason and leaves home, using a pilgrimage to St. Lorentz as an excuse. An old procuress had told him that a silly girl was deeply in love with him and wished to see him; but, just as he was lying down with her on clean linen sheets, he was set upon by four *Unger,* who beat him with oaken staves. Hanns finally talks himself out of the impasse, but only after parting from half his possessions, and returns to his wife at Bruneck for a proper scolding. As in the previous song, Oswald concludes that anyone who trusts old women is taking the devil as a wife and that they should be thrown into a lake. He even hopes that this old sorceress will be burned at the stake as a witch.

Scholars disagree as to the meaning of the four *Unger.* These could have been men of that name, which was not rare at the time in the area of St. Lorentz and Bruneck; they may actually have been Hungarians; or they could have been gypsies. Oswald, who abhorred Hungary, may have used the word *Unger* as an abusive term for any detestable person. The nationality of these men depends upon the meaning of their greeting, *Viegga waniadat,* which has been interpreted as Magyar and also as Romansch, which was then spoken in the immediate area. It is most probable that this poem and *Ain burger und ain hofman* were written at the same time, since they are both set in the Puster Valley and both damn old hags and suggest that they should be drowned.

Except for the traditional sin of *zubri* listed in his confession, this is Oswald's only reference to witchcraft, which suggests that he was less superstitious than most of his contemporaries. But in his day it took little more than Oswald's pious wish to burn a witch. Any inquisitive inquisitor who happened to overhear such a remark might well have reported his suspicions to his superior. The Holy Office would then have asked the old woman the *peinliche Frage,* which could be translated as either the "penal" question or the "painful" question. Prompted by suggestive questions and a few turns of the rack, the old hag would eventually confess to what was suggested. Then the church, too merciful to take a life, would turn her over to the lay authorities to be burned, perhaps after cutting off her right hand to prevent her from casting a spell from the pyre. To see how easily all this could be done, one needs only read the *Malleus maleficarum,* or *Witches' Hammer,* a manual for witch hunting written thirty-nine years after Oswald's death by two Dominicans and authorized by the papal bull *Summaris desideruntes affectibus.*

Oswald's unhappy Hauenstein song was followed by another disconsolate winter song, *Von trauren möcht ich werden taub,* a lament usually ascribed to the year 1429, at which time Oswald was still feuding with Bishop Ulrich of Brixen. The mood is much like that pervading the Hauenstein song: the poet is isolated in his snowbound castle, commiserating with himself and blaming his wife and children for his financial worries. This time Oswald seems to be under siege by angry peasants; and, despite his new connection with the *Feme,* he dares not go to Brixen because of his feud with Bishop Ulrich. Oswald upbraids the bishop, whom he derisively calls the "little unnamed one," for carrying on a love affair; and he warns him to cause no trouble. As in the Hauenstein song, he again lists the scenes of his earlier joys, this time the cities of Cologne, Vienna, Mainz, Paris, Avignon, Constance, and Nuremberg,[1] in order to contrast them with the misery he is now enjoying with his wife and children; and he implores his lord from Austria *(mein herr von Österreich)* to help him in his need. Thus, this is another petitional song composed to win sympathy and help. The "lord from Austria" must mean Frederick, who was an Austrian Hapsburg before becoming duke of Tyrol.

By this time, Frederick too was having strained relations with Bishop Ulrich.

There is one controversial allusion in this song, namely, to a *winderklaub* that has just returned to his old quarters near the Hauenstein. Some scholars believe this to be the name of a peasant who has been stationed there by Oswald's enemies to keep him under surveillance; and as evidence they cite the documented existence of a nearby peasant farm of that name, as well as the statement, in v. 6, that he is situated there *durch mangen spür,* which they understand to mean "for much spying." Other scholars believe that the *winderklaub* is the name of a cold wind, since Oswald says that it has brought cold, frost, deep snow, and a frozen stream from Bösaier's house, which must have been located at a greater altitude.

Since Oswald was so clever in speaking on two levels, perhaps he is making a play on words by associating the peasant's name with the local name of a wind. He uses this same technique with regard to the name of Bösaier, who was another of his neighbors, apparently a man wealthy enough to pay nine ducats for two oxen, as Margaret reports in a letter written to Oswald shortly before his death.[2] Despite his misery, Oswald did not miss his chance to make a pun on this peasant's name, which he expounds as *bös* (bad) and *aier* (eggs), in saying that no bird's heat ever hatched good fruit from a bad egg. Margaret's scribe had spelled the name as Pasayer, which shows that Oswald may have taken some liberty with the pronunciation of the name in making his pun.

Two of Oswald's songs can be attributed, with some degree of justification, to the year 1431. The first of these, *O wunnikliches paradies,* is a *Städtelob,* or eulogy of a city. Surprisingly enough, it praises the city of Constance, the very city that had caused Oswald such woe sixteen years earlier. It celebrates a very festive occasion; for the patricians of Constance had just regained control of the city, which they had recently lost to the up-and-coming guildsmen. Having returned to power with the aid of the Imperial army, the old rulers are celebrating their victory in the Katze, a dance hall erected in 1424. The other song, *Für allen schimpf,* is also a *Städtelob,* which praises the great city of Nuremberg. This song, built around different meanings of the word *hader,* remained unintelligible until Müller finally solved the puzzle by noting that *hader* was a much used and abused local term meaning tournament, love play, dancing, and various other things. Such a song could, of course, be amusing only as long as the word *hader* was in vogue. We know that Oswald attended an Imperial Diet at Nuremberg in 1431; but that hardly seemed the occasion for such a jolly song, since the empire was being sorely pressed by the Hussites and was disastrously defeated at the Battle of Taus on August 14. As we have seen, the song *Von trauren möcht ich werden taub,* presumably written in 1429, had included Nuremberg among the cities in which Oswald had previously enjoyed himself; so it may have been on some earlier occasion that he composed his *hader* song.

Two songs stem from the year 1432, when Oswald was in Italy accompanying Sigismund on his way to his coronation in Rome.[3] The first of these songs, *Wer die ougen wil verschüren,* defames Lombardy, where one can eat badly with good teeth, where dirt is deep and bread is dear, and where one daily finds ungodly penitence and false sincerity, which are two foods that Oswald cannot chew. The second strophe, composed in a lighter vein, is obscure to us because we no longer catch all the personal allusions. If anyone wishes to buy pickerel *(hechten)* by the pound, especially one with a liver weighing a stone, he should look in the emperor's chancelry, where you can catch such fish. This seems to allude to the secretary, Herman Hecht, who must have been a corpulent man, perhaps a heavy drinker too, since large livers betrayed great thirst. It is also probable that Hecht spoke a North German or *Plattdeutsch* dialect, for the last line of the strophe calls him a *sütten hechtigin,* which is a Low German equivalent of the High German *süsses Hechtlein* or "sweet little pickerel." [4]

The third strophe speaks humorously of Herman Hecht, Marquart Brisacher, and Oswald's uncle *(öheim),* who would be better off with pretty girls in Constance and Ulm than losing their money in Piacenza. Here Oswald is alluding to the good times he and Sigismund's other retainers had the previous year in the Swabian cities after leaving the diet at Nuremberg. Oswald also alludes to the trouble his poor memory is causing his scribe, who, it might be added, probably wrote the beautiful MS B. The very enigmatic fourth strophe compares a certain Sebastian to an ox. It is clear that this song, like so many of Oswald's, was aimed at the initiated few. As we shall see in the next song, the "uncle" may have been Matthew Schlick, a very important dignitary, whom Oswald called "Uncle" even though they were not related.

Oswald had the good fortune to be relieved of his boredom at Piacenza when Sigismund moved on to Parma, where Oswald remained until being sent with Master Nicolas Stock on a mission to the Council of Basel on May 30. During their stay in Parma, Oswald and his friends received the news that some of Sigismund's envoys to Rome had been attacked and seriously beaten at Ronciglione by a party of Italians under a certain Count Dulce. The report may have been an objective and official communiqué, or perhaps it was delivered, in part, by the victims. Oswald has made a lively and dramatic account of the incident by using the techniques of the *Landsknechtlied* or *soldatesca* song. It begins:

Es komen neue mer gerant	a
von ainem graven, süess genant,	a
wie sawer der sein gesst emphacht	b
dort im Runzelian.	c
Hinfür den babst gelangt der schal,	d
zu Rom für mangen cardinal,	d
daraus so ward ain grosser bracht	b
von weiben und auch man.	c
Die kirweich was bestalt	e
von pawern und von knappen;	f
die herberg si da buchten auff	w
und lieffen an die trappen	f
mit keulen, spiessen wolbetracht	b
auff ainen bösen wan.	c
Sechzehen gesst gezalt	e
die bischof wolten weihen;	g
und welcher da kain beulen hett,	w
der dorft sein nicht zu leihen.	g
Beraiter vier für ain gemacht,	b
ettlicher bracht der van.	c

New tidings are arriving about a count named Sweet, and how sourly he receives his guests in Ronciglione. The noise has reached the Pope and many cardinals in Rome; and from it has arisen a great tumult of men and women. The church was consecrated by peasants and workers. They broke open the inn and rushed up the stairs with malicious intent and well supplied with clubs and spears. The bishops wished to consecrate sixteen guests all told; and, if any of them had no contusions, he was unable to lend any, for many a one took away with him four times as many as he had given (?).[5]

As is so often the case, Oswald makes a pun on a name, this time translating Count Dulce as Count Sweet, who greets his guests sourly. Like many humorous songs of the time, particularly those in the Neidhart and the *Landsknechtlied* traditions, this one uses the word for a church consecration *(kirchweih)* in order to denote a brawl. Anyone familiar with Pieter Breughel the Elder's kermess paintings can well imagine that such rustic dancing and drunken merriment often ended in bloody squabbles; and we know that the word kermess *(kirchweih)* immediately suggested bloodshed to Oswald's audience. Since the Italian attackers are doing the consecrating, they are called the "bishops."

In the following four strophes Oswald gives a blow-by-blow account of the brawl in which his former colleagues are so severely mauled; and he shows more amusement than pity, even for his "uncle" Matthew Schlick, whose nose was severely damaged in the fray. In fact he displays malicious joy in depicting their various breaks and bruises. Oswald does not actually describe all the action but sometimes describes the injuries in detail and only briefly reports how they were inflicted. Two members of the party, Sir Gottschalk and Sir Mert of Speyer, had to wear slings, he says, that made their arms look like lyres; and there is reason to suppose that they may have related part of the story themselves (105/47). Resuming the metaphor of the *kirchweih,* which he also calls a *kirchtag,* Oswald contends that those who were not thrown down at least two flights of stairs were not fully consecrated, and those who were not clubbed had not truly confessed.

There may be some truth to Oswald's statement in *Wer die ougen will verschüren* that his faulty memory was causing his scribe trouble; for it is quite possible that the latter was then preparing MS B of his songs. In any case, the caption to the manuscript states it was composed and completed *(geticht und volbracht)* by Oswald von Wolkenstein, knight of the most illustrious Roman king, Sigismund, on the first Sunday after St. Augustine's Day, 1432. It is most likely that the scribe had MS A before him when he wrote down those songs that had appeared in it, a few of which he himself had originally written down; but he probably wrote the eighteen new ones, as well as the two now under discussion, from dictation. Oswald still called Sigismund "Roman king," because he had not yet acquired his longed-for title of emperor, for which he had to wait some nine months longer, until May 31, 1433.

Another bit of evidence that Oswald and the scribe were at work on MS B during his exile in Piacenza is the fact that the manuscript is adorned with a portrait of exactly the same size as the MS painted by an Italian artist, putatively by Pisanello, who also painted one of Sigismund. This portrait is notable as being the first truly realistic picture of any German poet. The illustration in MS A, which shows Oswald dressed up in all his finery, is also an actual likeness and even shows his empty eyesocket. Thus it differs from the earlier miniatures of Walther and the other minnesingers, which, being posthumous, were idealized, stylized, and interchangeable figments of the artist's imagination. Nevertheless, it fails to give such facial detail as is found in the illustration to MS B or to express Oswald's firm, resolute, and ruthless character.

Two more songs may be authoritatively assigned to Oswald's later life. One of these, a *passio* (story of Christ's suffering) beginning *In oberland*, was completed in 1436, as its caption attests. The other, *Mich fragt ain ritter*, is a long and tedious treatise concerning the law composed in 1438. Since many of Oswald's religious and didactic songs cannot be dated, it seems advisable to group them thematically rather than try to arrange them chronologically. They will be the subject of our next two sections.

II *Didactic Songs*

Whereas Oswald seems to have composed religious songs throughout his life, most of his truly didactic ones appear to have been written nearer its end. To be sure, he had often given good advice, usually in the form of proverbs and proverbial sayings, such as the adage that parents should chastise their children; yet his irresistible urge to educate other people seems to have started later, perhaps after he himself had become responsible for bringing up children of his own. In most cases, the lesson he taught is the theme of the entire song; but sometimes it merely intrudes into an otherwise self-sufficient work. This is true, for example, of *Zergangen ist meins herzen we,* which is a happy counterpart to the melancholy winter song *Von trauren möcht ich werden taub*. Although this song begins as a May song, it is thoroughly personal and subjective. Oswald's sorrow is subsiding now that the snow is finally melting on Seiser Alb and at Flack and the water is running down from Kastelruth into the Eisack, as he has heard his neighbor Mosmair saying. The birds are singing in Oswald's forest around Hauenstein, and he is inclined to sing no matter what other people may think. He invites all people, and even the wild animals, to rejoice with him in the beautiful season.

But suddenly the carefree mood changes. Oswald cites the proverb that righteous behavior is a great treasure because everything comes to light. Sir Christian in the upper parish is no fool, and you have to get up early to trick him. He bides his time, but not for long, before "confirming" (i.e., striking) your cheek so that you forget your evil and can no longer laugh. Some scholars actually thought that Sir Christian was a minister in some highland parish, but anyone familiar with Oswald's anthropomorphic concepts of God realizes that he was a personification of the Deity.

The most popular form of didacticism in the fourteenth and fifteenth centuries was that of allegory; and much of the literature of the time consists of interminable narratives in which abstractions, represented by abstract ladies with their abstract handmaidens, hold endless conversations about right and wrong, good and evil, and other moral matters. Religious allegory had also served as a model for amorous allegory, and numerous allegorical figures were created to represent the virtues and vices of love. As a sensual man of action, Oswald avoided such abstractions almost entirely; for he preferred ladies made of flesh and blood to those made of philosophical concepts.

One of Oswald's rare excursions into allegory is his song *O rainer got,* which more or less follows a tradition popular since Walther. After praising God with a fine selection of His most flowery epithets, Oswald laments that He is so mocked in this world, where shame pushes ahead of honor and injustice perverts justice. Anyone who can do that thinks himself very clever; for it is taught in the princes' school, where many a chair pushes ahead of the tables and benches, even if it would only be a stool if weighed according to its honor. Whereas most allegorists visualized their virtues and vices as handsome ladies, this song uses three pieces of furniture to symbolize how petty men of no virtue are pushing their way ahead of better-born men at court.[6] In the second strophe, Oswald detects three animals in this world. Two of these, loyalty and honor *(treu und er)*, are seldom pursued, whereas the third, falsity *(falsch)*, is allowed no rest. Wherever loyalty and honor live in the forest, they seek each other out, just as falsity seeks out evil *(bös)*. Wicked people may thrive in this world, but the supreme Prince of Heaven will give the comfort of His Kingdom only to those who strive for honor; and honor is better than any prince's treasures.

Perhaps the least impressive of Oswald's songs is *Wer hie umb diser welde lust*, a paraphrase of the immensely popular *Bescheidenheit*, a thirteenth-century aphoristic work by a peripatetic poet known as Freidank. Most of the sixty rhyming couplets are based on Freidank's far longer work; but Oswald may have chosen those ideas concurring with his current frame of mind. Being sixty-one years old—a ripe age at that time—he is mindful of his own mortality and preaches that the joys of this world are not worth the dangers which the soul incurs through them. As on other occasions, he particularly warns against becoming beholden to princes; and he also warns against the pleasures of wine, anger, gambling, and women. The song consists largely of pithy platitudes praising virtue, damning vice, and explaining human nature. Much of this wisdom is derived from the Bible, particularly from those parts then attributed to Solomon, but also from popular folk wisdom.

Oswald never tired of condemning the pleasures of this world, which he describes as snares on man's way to salvation; and he calls upon his fellows to turn away from worldly joys (*dein willen ker von irdischem gelust*, 4/6). Like Walther before him, he compares the world to a tavern keeper who will demand full payment on the final day of reckoning (7/26–30); and, therefore, he believes that no one who really knew the joys of the world would buy them quickly (9/5–6). We have seen that all three of Oswald's major autobiographical songs ended by rejecting the world. His farewell to youth concludes with the regret that he has served the world instead of doing good works (18/108–110), his Perpignan song concludes that on Judgment Day a clothes bag will be worth no more than a purse and a belfry no more than a vinegar jug and that it would be better for us if we had guarded our soul (19/217–24), and the last strophe of the song of the seven mortal dangers proclaims the vanity of worldly life (23/129–160).

In addition to these numerous intrusions of *contemptus mundi* (contempt for the world) in his other songs, Oswald composed one entire song on that theme, namely *O welt, o welt*. This intensely personal outcry from crushing captivity includes many traditional elements of *Weltabkehr* (rejection of the world). The song is well summarized in the second half of the fourth strophe:

> Seid uns in diser kranken zeit
> all werltlich freud neur pringet laid
> und süess ain sauer ende,
> und aller lust auf erd die leng verdriessen pringt,
> so wundert mich, worumb der mensch nach freuden ringt.
> Offt, weiser man, wie wirstu plind
> in aller kunst behende! (9/54–60)

Since in these fragile times all worldly joy brings us only sorrow, sweetness has a sour ending, and all our pleasure here on earth brings ultimate vexation, I marvel why men strive for pleasure. Wise man skilled in all the arts, how often you grow blind!

The most "scientific" of Oswald's works is his astrological treatise, *Des grossen herren wunder*, in which he explains the influence of the constellations upon man's features and his character.[7] Man's birth is affected by the seven planets: the sun, the moon, Mars, Mercury, Jupiter, Venus, and Saturn, in combination with the twelve signs of the Zodiac: Lion, Crab, Scorpion, Bull, Ram, Virgins, Twins, Fish, Archer, Balance, Aquarius, and Goat. Consequently, Oswald should have eighty-four combinations; but he simplifies his scheme and shortens his song by relating each planet to only one or two signs, allowing sixteen verses to each planet. It would be hard to find a physical or moral trait he has not covered.

From our modern point of view, there is something tragic about the faith in astrology, which diverted so much intellectual energy from more rewarding endeavors. Since almost no one questioned astrological prognostication, it is not surprising that much thought and study were dedicated to it. Nearly two centuries after Oswald's death, astrology was still reputable enough for Wallenstein, the most powerful general of the Thirty Years' War, to let himself be paralyzed into inaction by the predictions of his court astrologer. We may be sure that many of Oswald's contemporaries were wrongfully judged because of the signs under which they were born or because of some physical feature astrally associated with moral faults. Total faith in stellar influence would, however, vitiate free will and thus undermine the Christian concept of sin. Oswald must have realized this fact; for he states that, even though the stars may have given a man evil inclinations, God has given him a certain nobility *(adel)* that will enable him to escape his blemish through diligent virtue and with the help of the Holy Cross.

As a member of the privileged class, Wolkenstein naturally believed that the social classes were preordained by God and should not be altered. We have seen that, excepting the wicked goose, all birds remain in the order into which God put them, whereas some men, represented by the recently discussed chairs, try to displace their betters (the tables and benches) at court. To the problem of the three orders ordained by God, Oswald devoted an entire song beginning *Ir babst, ir kaiser, du pawman,* in which he enjoins the pope, the emperor, and the peasants to remain in their order as cleric, nobleman, and worker. It is the duty of the pope to pray day and night for Christendom, while clerics should pray devoutly to God, who created all things and redeemed us with His own death, which He suffered incarnate on the cross. The emperor and all other men consecrated to the sword should uphold justice and the faith and should particularly protect widows, orphans, the poor and the rich; and they should shed their own blood rather than let anyone reproach them and besmirch their honor. He who is born to work should work loyally; for, if he does not, he will lose his work both here and there. On the other hand, if he is loyal, as suits a peasant, and dies with real penitence, he shall have eternal joy there. Oswald then calls upon all the orders, to wit: princes, counts, knights, squires, burghers, peasants, cardinals, bishops, and simple prelates, all clerics and laymen to do right in this world.

This song follows the ancient literary topos of the three estates: clerics, knights, and peasants *(pfaffen, ritter, und gebûr).* By Oswald's day this triadic division of society was no longer valid;

because the bourgeoisie had gained an important, if unrecognized, place in society, as Oswald must have realized when Sabina married a rich burgher rather than a poor nobleman. But literary traditions die hard; and literature continued to divide society into priests, knights, and peasants, even after the bourgeoisie had produced many important patrons. It will be noted that Oswald either ignored the burghers or included them with the peasants as workers *(arbaiter)*. Oswald did not scorn menial work, at least not for menial people. When his disdainful heroines send their rustic suitors back to their agrarian chores, he is not ridiculing productive work but rather the impudent peasants who, born to work, are trying to ape the customs of the upper classes.

Like other country gentlemen, Oswald was quite blind to the material progress then being made in the cities. The arts and sciences of the ancient world, which had been precariously preserved by the monasteries, were flourishing anew; and innovations were steadily appearing in medicine and chemistry as well as in agriculture, horticulture, mining, metallurgy, and other branches of production. The accumulation of capital made large industrial and mercantile operations possible; and the increased social recognition and political power enjoyed by the artisan guilds gave their members a professional pride clearly reflected in the high quality of their products. As Gerhard Eis has shown, the German language was rapidly becoming an effective medium for advancing and disseminating scientific and technological knowledge.[8] Naturally, none of this economic ferment is revealed by Oswald's songs.

Oswald's longest work, beginning *Mich fragt ain ritter*, expounds his views on the law. This treatise cannot be called a song, since it has no melody and is to be read. He himself calls it a *fabula*, or a kind of didactic poem, which would have been called a *rede* in the vernacular. It has almost no esthetic merit, being composed in the simple four-stressed rhyming couplets then customary for such lectures and sermons as well as for straightforward narratives. The poetic "I" is presented as an old man, whom a knight asks to explain why, although justice has been ordained for everyone in Christendom, it is so seldom carried out according to "imperial" law.

The old man replies that many heads are guilty of the miscarriage of justice. No matter how clever a ruler is, he can be fooled unless he has a wise council, in which Dame Honor is at home, and unless he follows its advice in the fear of the Lord. Throughout the world, violence has driven out justice; for, when the abbot carries dice, all the brothers play too in order to please their master. Vicedomos, counselors, governors, court bailiffs, judges, advocates, justices, and constables all walk a false path to please their superior. Since this poem has 410 verses, it is too long to be analyzed in detail. Suffice it to say that Oswald deplores bribery, false witness, trickery, ignorant judges, and crooked advocates. He is especially strongly opposed to judicial power in ecclesiastical hands. St. Peter had only one sword when he struck Malchus' servant; but now the clerics wish to wield both swords, the temporal as well as the spiritual, and there is less equity where they rule than in lands ruled by secular princes. At this point, Oswald summarizes his views on clerics, nobles, and workers as revealed in his previously discussed song; and he expresses the wish that clerics would keep to their order, since they cause more strife than all laymen taken together. In Rome he has seen how law and justice are perverted through trickery and simony by those who should shine as our examples but have neither fear of God nor sense of shame.

Wherever imperial law *(kaiserliches recht)* obtains, Oswald prefers written law (*gsatzte recht*, 112/218); but common law is also to be respected. Imperial law is superior to common law; since the emperor is the source of all law, and no territorial law can do without it. No matter how old it is, common law is to be avoided if bad and should be reformed. For how can an illiterate peasant understand the law better than a trained jurist? And why do people often appoint a stupid judge who lacks fear of the Lord and wise counsel? A prince should have noble, wise, and conscientious advisers, or his justice will fail. In addition to offering these and may other platitudes about justice, Oswald is more specific in saying that he considers written law superior to customary law, and he also prefers a verdict by twelve jurors to that rendered by the whole community. When Oswald mentions imperial law *(kaiserliches recht)*, he is referring specifically to the *Schwabenspiegel* (Mirror of the Swabians), a law code valid in most of South Germany, which was much influenced by Roman law.[10]

Oswald signs this *fabula* with his own name, and rightly so; for it seems to express his personal views. His opposition to ecclesiastical jurisdiction may well reflect his long feud with the bishop of Brixen, whose arbitration concerning Hauenstein he refused to accept. As a wealthy man who could afford the services of jurists trained in Latin and in Roman law, he naturally welcomed the *Rezeption*, or adoption of the latter, which was just then beginning to displace the ancient customary law as the law of the land.[11] In the old Germanic days every man had been his own lawyer, the law being a simple oral code that could be learned by attending lawsuits; and even an illiterate peasant might be a shrewd advocate at court. Roman law was first introduced only in order to clarify certain fine points insufficiently covered by the native oral law, but unscrupulous advocates gradually learned to quibble over trivial points in order to consult Roman law and thus disqualify their unlettered opponents. This procedure naturally played into the hands of the greater lords, who used it to dispossess and disfranchise not only the peasants but also the lesser nobles who could neither learn the new law nor afford to retain well-trained legal assistants. Oswald may allude to such unscrupulous legal practices in his *winderklaub* song, when he accuses Bishop Ulrich of using *welischer vernufft* (foreign reason, 104/54). Whereas the new Roman law, being codified, was far more efficient and had universal validity, it brought with it the barbaric and illogical Roman practice of applying torture to elicit confessions, so that the most innocent person could be persuaded to confess to heresy, witchcraft, or other offenses with suitable leading questions.

To all appearances, one of Oswald's last didactic songs was his *Und swig ich nu,* in which he chastises the "twelve drunkennesses." In this case, he does not seem to be following his own convictions, which are better expressed in his jolly drinking songs, but rather a Latin original, which has been preserved in a manuscript from Sterzing in South Tyrol. In the opening verse Oswald admits quite frankly that he is singing this song because people would soon forget him if he remained silent. He then describes in detail twelve types of behavior resulting from immoderate indulgence. Although this is an *Alterslied,* or song from old age, it is very skilfully composed, the meter and rhymes are smooth, and the descriptions are very vivid.

III *Religious Songs*

Men of the late Middle Ages made less distinction than we do between the sacred and the profane; all secular life was imbued with religion while, conversely, all religion had strong worldly ingredients. We notice, for example, that music was not distinguished as being either sacred or profane; one could use the same melody for songs of divine or of erotic love, and a single description of feminine perfection could suit both the Virgin Mary and one's mistress. Consequently, it is not always possible to know whether one of Oswald's songs is sacred or profane. Besides, many songs that are predominantly worldly in content may begin with a devout invocation or end with a prayer, or pious little platitudes may be inserted in it. It is usually assumed that poets write most of their sacred verses late in life, after the world has lost its charm and their souls are preparing for doomsday. This seems to be true to a certain degree of Oswald, if we take quantity as our measure; yet his most moving religious songs were composed, as we have seen, in the middle of his life while he was in prison. While aware of the provident and merciful God expounded by St. Augustine, Boethius, St. Francis of Assisi, and others, Oswald seems to have embraced the popular piety of his apocalyptic age in fearing an austere and unapproachable God. This distant Deity may have resulted not only from Greek philosophy, for example from the concept of the Unmoved Mover of Aristotle's *Metaphysics*, but also from the administrative situation of the late Roman and Byzantine empires, where the emperor lived in seclusion like an oriental despot and was seldom accessible to his subjects. Unable to take their petitions directly to the emperor, his subjects had to persuade his officials, through bribery or otherwise, to intercede on their behalf. It is not surprising that people accustomed to such governmental practices would apply similar methods to their religion and that it became customary for Christians to seek intercession, through either their priests or the saints in heaven.

Oswald's God is a God almighty (*almächtiger got,* 126/33). He is powerful (*reich,* 9/64, 35/13), the All-highest (*dem allerhöchsten,* 10/34), a Lord of might (*ain herr der mächtigkait,* 95/6), a high King who rules in power (*ain hoher küng, gewaltikleich gesessen,* 111/2), and a powerful King on heaven's throne (*gewaltiklicher küng der himel tröne,* 7/2) whose lordly might rules all power (*sein herrlich krafft herscht aller macht volkomenlich allmächtig,* 111/19). He is a Prince (*fürst,* 27/82), Prince of all lords (*fürst aller herren,* 35/14), Master of all princes (*maister aller fürsten,* 36/13), the Prince of heaven (*der himel fürst,* 29/1), the highest Prince (*der höchste fürst* (114/48), and the Supreme Prince of Heaven (*obrist himelfürst,* 95/51). He is an exalted King (*hochgelobte küng,* 111/56), a King of all realms (*küng aller reich,* 35/13), a King of kings (*küng aller küng,* 111/129), and Lord of lords (*herr aller herren,* 111/130). Needless to say, such a King is without beginning or end (*an anefangk noch end,* 6/38); and He and His Kingdom are eternal (*der immer lebt an end,* 14/6; *ewig lebt,* 31/3; *ewigs reich,* 7/6). From Germanic and feudal tradition, medieval men had inherited an image of God as a feudal overlord, and it will be noted that Oswald always uses the word *lehen* (to enfeoff, give in fee) in referring to God's granting of life or other goods (2/6, 8/31). We should remember that all of Oswald's standing epithets for the Godhead had been imported to Europe together with Christianity. In fact, all of his professions of faith are strictly orthodox. This can be demonstrated by relating them to the Apostles' Creed, which summarizes the chief articles of faith in the following sequence:

> I believe in God the Father Almighty, Maker of heaven and earth: and in Jesus Christ His only son our Lord: who was conceived by the Holy Ghost, Born of the Virgin Mary: suffered under Pontius Pilate, was crucified, dead, and buried: He descended into hell; the third day He rose again from the dead: He ascended into heaven, and sitteth on the right hand of God the Father Almighty: From thence He shall come to judge the quick and the dead. I believe in the Holy Ghost: The holy Catholic Church; The Communion of Saints: The Forgiveness of sins: The Resurrection of the body: and the Life everlasting.

Oswald often refers to God as the Maker of heaven and earth. He is a Creator (*schepfer,* 6/54) and a Maker of all creation (*ain schaffer aller creatur,* 36/13), who has given us body and soul (*der dir dein leib und sel verlihen hat,* 2/6) and ordains each man's lot with His holy hand (*der jedem sein gesatz wäglichen misst mit seiner heilgen hand,* 1/65). He created not only heaven and earth but also leaves and grass (*der himel, erd schuoff, laub und gras,* 111/45) and gave colors to the sun, moon, and flowers (*den geit er farb und liechten glanz,* 2/15). As Oswald explains in a long strophe, God keeps and protects heaven, earth, the water, stones, fish, birds, mountains, forests, worms, and ravens (2/19–36). It is not surprising, therefore, that all nature praises God, as we learn from the first two strophes of his song *Du armer mensch,* which begins as follows:

Du armer mensch, las dich dein sünd hie reuen ser.	a
O hailger gaist, gib uns deins heiligen vatters ler,	a
das ich bedenck ain klain die macht und wirdig er	a
in meim gesangk von got, dem nicht geleichet.	b
Neun kör der engel, die loben got an underlast.	c
In lobt die sunn, der man und aller sterne glast.	c
In lobt der himel, der alles wesen umbetast,	c
und was dorinn regniert, sein namen reichet.	b
Perg und ouch tal, des voglin schal, der visch im wag,	eed
all würm und tier, geloubet mir, was ich eu sag,	ffd
laub, gras, gevild, das wasser wild, die nacht, der tag	ggd
erkennt und lobt got, dem der teufel weichet.	b

Poor man, repent of your sins here. O Holy Ghost, give us your Holy Father's teaching so that I will remember in my song the power and worthy honor of God, whom nothing equals. Nine choirs of angels praise God without cease. He is praised by the sun and moon, and the brightness of all the stars. He is praised by heaven, which encompasses all beings; and all that dwells therein exalts his name. Hill and dale, the songs of the birds, the fish in the wave, all worms and beasts, believe me what I say, leaves, grass, and fields, the wild water, night and day recognize and praise God, from Whom the devil retreats.

This panegyric continues in the next strophe, which tells how all living creatures recognize God, and how even the stones broke asunder when the Creator was crucified. The plants of the earth praise God through their blossoms and timely fruit. Although a man were favored with all skill and were ever so famous, he could not possibly, even to save his life, fittingly describe the very least of these flowers. The third strophe tells us that, whereas all creatures in the water and air and on the earth are thankful to the Lord of Majesty for having created them, only man is not, even though he was made in God's image and given dominion over all beasts and fruits. The remaining two strophes take up the theme that only man is ungrateful and dishonors God, despite the fact that He is almighty and can punish with hell's fire; and it ends with an admonition to repent sins here and resist the devil with God's help. Many of these motifs are repeated in a *Danklied* beginning *Der oben swebt,* which glorifies God for having created the skies, the earth, and the waters and states that all living creatures thank him for creating them.

Since God must punish man's ingratitude, He is not only a king but also a judge. He is an avenger of wicked works (*ain recher böse werche macht,* 95/5), who pays in kind (*gelt wider gelt, got selber melt,* 32/13). Since man persists in his sinful ways despite his free will (the previously mentioned *adel* that God gave him for resisting the stars), God feels great wrath (*zoren,* 29/10). God's ingenuity in making the punishment fit the crime is depicted in the song *Durch toren weis,* which describes the horrors of hell as they had appeared in visions of the Otherworld and somewhat as Dante described them in his *Inferno.* But God also chastises here and now, as was shown by the great signs manifested in France, England, and elsewhere and mentioned in the Hussite song (27/85). We have also seen that Oswald accepted his own captivity as a divine punishment (1/13). He repeated this thought in his song about the mortal dangers he was exposed to, which says that he was so badly treated by his sweetheart because God, from His high throne, leaves nothing unpunished (*Got lat nicht ungestraffet von seinem höchsten stuol,* 23/113).

God is not only an avenger of evil but also a rewarder of good works (*ain loner guoter dinge,* 95/4). Oswald, therefore, regrets that he has not performed good works (*neur guote werck, ob ich der hett gemert,* 6/36), and he knows that we can take nothing with us when we die except these good works (*und uns nicht volgt, wann unsre guote werck gar blos,* 9/73; *das mir nicht scheiner volgt wan meiner berche zol,* 18/110). God is also a God of love, and all love comes from Him (*Wer liebe trait ze got, von dem si kompt, daran si hafftet,* 4/8). He wishes to be loved (*er wil der liebst gehalden sein,* 1/69), and he can even be compelled by love to show mercy (*lieb got den herren twinget,* 1/76). God is a vessel of superabundant mercy that no one can exhaust (*vas der barmung uberfluss, das niemand kan erschepfen,* 36/25–

26); and Oswald begs Him, through His great divine mercy (*all dein barmung göttlich gross*, 6/39), to guard him against Lucifer and his fellows.

In view of Oswald's great supernatural dread and awe before the Lord of Wrath, it is surprising that he follows the mores of his age in sometimes treating Him quite frivolously. His concept of God being strongly anthropomorphic, he sometimes refers to Him in human terms. We have seen that God is the pastor of the upper parish who can "confirm" your cheek, and we also learn that He is the only man (*got, der ainig man*, 6/17) who can save Oswald from the punishment due him because of his sins. Likewise, He is the man and master (*man, maister*, 120/16, 19) who has fashioned the lady whom Oswald admires. In other words, Oswald's theology was on about the same cultural level as the current musical hit "Put your hand in the hand of the man" (who stilled the waters).

Oswald believes not only in God, but also in "His only son our Lord." Whereas some writers distinguish between the wrathful and jealous God of the Old Testament and the loving Jesus of the New Testament, Oswald does not seem to make this distinction often or clearly; and for him even the Son can be a God of Wrath:

> O heilger Crist, seit das dein macht ist ungezalt,
> so wundert mich ob allem wunder manigvalt,
> das wir nicht fürchten ser dein zorniklich gestalt
> und grosse plag, die du uns macht beweisen. (8/49–52)

O holy Christ, since Thy might is untold, I marvel above all marvels that we do not greatly fear Thy wrathful figure and the great affliction that Thou canst inflict upon us.

One might say that God the Father and God the Son are clearly distinguished only when Jesus is a babe in the manger with the ox and the ass, as He is described in the Christmas carol *In Suria ain braiten hal* (35/25). Such a song might well have been inspired by a painting of the nativity, or else by a crèche. What seemed to amaze Oswald most in the nativity was that Jesus was not only Mary's son but also her Lord and father (*ir herr du was, got, vatter und si dein muotter*, 35/29). The same wonderment is expressed in the song *Wach, menschlich tier*, which speaks of

God's child as being his mother's father (*der seiner muotter vatter ist,* 2/24).

God, in the person of the Son, is most remembered as the one who died for our sins; and Oswald wishes to suffer patiently in honor of the bitter martyrdom He suffered (*gedultiklich ich leiden wil ze eren der bitter marter, so du laid,* 7/8). Through His suffering on the cross, He redeems us if we do not displease Him (24/69–72). Christ's other great service was the harrowing of hell (*er brach die hell, die nie gefros,* 2/11; *die hell er brach,* 31/11; *zerbrechen schier die vinstern keich mit seiner aigen hande, und die gerechten darauss holt,* 111/27). The harrowing of hell, in which Jesus emptied hell of all those Old Testament prophets and good pre-Christian pagans, is not mentioned in canonical Scripture but came to Western Europe in the apocryphal Gospel of Nicodemus, perhaps the most popular of all Scriptures. The harrowing of hell was a favorite subject of art and was often included in the Easter plays of Oswald's time.

In 1436 Oswald composed a long song, his longest, which begins *In oberlant* and relates Christ's passion, that is, His suffering between Gethsemane and Golgotha. This *passio* tells how, because Adam and Eve had caused God to lose His whole army of men and women, God sent his Son to earth to redeem them by dying on the cross. After three introductory strophes, the narrative proper begins with Christ's betrayal by Judas. We see Him seized and bound by the Jews and taken to the judge's house, where Peter denies Him thrice. We also witness Mary's agony as her Son is led to Caiaphas and Pilate and then to Herod. After being ridiculed, He is led back to Pilate, who caters to the Jews by having Him flogged and having a crown of thorns placed on His head. As soon as Christ has been mocked with the greeting "Hail the King of the Jews," Pilate washes his hands of the affair to free himself of blame; and Christ has to carry his heavy cross to Calvary, where Mary hears the three nails being hammered into his hands and feet. Before dying, Christ cries out "My God, my God, why hast Thou forsaken me? Into Thy hands I commend my spirit." The blind Jew, Longinus, then comes with a spear and pierces Him in his side; and the blood and water that run down the spear make him see again.

This account differs little from the Biblical one, except for the references to the harrowing of hell, the blind Jew Longinus, and the plucking of Christ's beard as a sign of indignity. Perhaps Oswald was inspired by some church mural depicting Christ's passion, or, more probably, he was merely describing a passion play he had witnessed, since many such spectacles were performed in his time. Like the passion plays, this song helped fan the hatred against the Jews as Christ killers. It does not mention that Jesus, Mary, and the apostles were also Jews, because they were not. Those who believed in Jesus were Christians, not Jews. In Oswald's day anti-Semitism was not a matter of race. The Jews were persecuted because of their false religion and their disloyalty to Jesus, not because of their race. Once a Jew saw his error and became a Christian, he no longer differed from other Christians; and many a Jewish soul was lovingly saved from eternal damnation by forced conversion, perhaps by means of fire, the rack, and convincing theological arguments. Otherwise the Jews must all suffer in the second chamber of hell along with heathens and heretics, as Oswald tells us (32/35).

According to the Apostles' Creed, Jesus was "conceived by the Holy Ghost," so Oswald naturally believed in it too, even if he may not have had much understanding for an abstract concept that could not be grasped in anthropomorphic terms. His song *O welt, o welt* ends with the prayer that the Holy Ghost convert him and his friends and turn them from sin; and his song *Du armer mensch* requests the Holy Ghost to give him his Holy Father's wisdom so that he can sing of His power and worthy honor (8/2). The seven gifts of the Holy Ghost include not only divine wisdom *(weisheit gots)* but also intellect or understanding *(vernufft und kunst),* counsel *(göttlicher rat),* fortitude *(gots sterk),* fear of the lord *(göttliche forcht),* knowledge *(göttliche kunst),* and piety *(göttliche lieb, guot),* which appear in Oswald's confession, *Mein sünd und schuld* (39/37–40). In a short table blessing, *Gesegnet sei die frucht,* Oswald prays to the Father, the Holy Ghost, and the Son to grant him mercy and save him from the devils (*Vatter, heiliger gaist, mit deinem sun uns gnad vollaist, und nicht den feinden gunn* (14/13–15).

Oswald seems to have been aware that the three persons of the Trinity are inseparable, in fact the same song declares that God, who is "three-in-one," suffered death (*selbdritt ain durch uns laid den tod,* 14/5). In the prayer *Der himel fürst uns heut bewar* he addresses a petition to the "Trinity, Son, Holy Ghost, enclosed in the form of a Father" (*Trivaltikait, sun, heilger gaist verslossen in ains vatters laist* (29/25). In *Der oben swebt,* a brief story of salvation, he refers to God as old and young and "thrice comprehended in one word" (*trilitzsch gefasst in ainlitz zung* 31/5); in *O welt, o welt* he asks God to help him in the strength of the Holy Trinity (*in kraft der heilgen trinitat,* 9/28), and in his didactic song *Wol auf und wacht* he advises men to serve the One and Three (*dem ainen und den dreien,* 118/57). In *Wolauff, als das zu himel sei* he asks Maria to help with the entire *trinitat* (15/19), and in *Wer ist, die da durchleuchtet* he praises Maria, who bore Christ, who was One in Three (*selb dreien freien unitas* (13/11).

Although Oswald accepted all dogma unquestioningly, it is clear that the Holy Ghost did not greatly excite his fancy. It is also evident that, despite the Divine Love occasionally attributed to God, Oswald recognized Him, both Father and Son, primarily as a god of wrath and vengeance. Knowing himself a poor human animal *(menschlich tier)* unable to resist the temptations of the flesh, he naturally feared for his immortal soul. This supernatural dread was greatest, as we have seen, during his first captivity, when he did not know where his poor soul might go (1/114). If a man has failed to love God, God will pursue him until he is caught in a snare (*er hengt im nach, bis in ain latz ergreifft,* 1/72), an image taken from the already described sport of *Heckenjagd,* or the driving of game into previously set nets.

Oswald's fear of death is convincingly expressed in the last strophe of his song *Loblicher got* (7/37–54), which he wrote in the dungeon of Vellenberg Castle during his third captivity, perhaps while still fearing that Frederick might execute him for treason.

Der sorgen raiff — a
hat meinen leib zesamen fest gebunden. — b
Von sorgen gross mein herz geswillt, — c
forcht, sorg, die hab ich funden. — b
Durch sorg mein houbt genzlích erschillt, — c
grausslíche sorg mir dick den slauf erwert. — d
Mit unbeswaiff — a
vier mauern dick mein trauren hand verslossen. — e
O lange nacht, ellénder tag, — f

eur zeit ist gar verdrossen! e
Vil mancher schrick kompt mir zu klag, f
dem laider hilf von mir wirt klain beschert. d
Gen dieser werlt hab ich die angst g
verschuldet sicher klain, h
neur umb den got, der mich vor langst g
beschuoff von Wolkenstein; h
der sei mein trost und aufenthalt! i
O Fellenberg, wie ist dein freud so kalt! i

The rope of care has bound my body tight. My heart is swelled with great anxiety; and fear and sorrow I have found. My head is wholly racked with great worries, and often gruesome fears dispel my sleep. Four solid walls have shut my sorrow in. Oh, lasting night, oh wretched day, your time is all vexation. Full many a fright I must lament, for which, alas, no help is granted me. Surely I have hardly earned this fear here in the world, but just from God alone, who long ago created me, von Wolkenstein. May He become my comfort and support! O Vellenberg, how cold your pleasure is!

It would be difficult to make a good translation of this song; because the English language has no equivalent for the word *Sorge,* as will have been discovered by anyone trying to english *Frau Sorge* in Goethe's *Faust.* Since no onc English word combines the concepts of care, anxiety, worry, and fear, I have used all of these to render Oswald's one word *sorge,* even though this expedient destroys the marvelous cffect of its battering-ram repetition in his song.

Oswald's fear of death is also vividly expressed in the song *Ich spür ain tier,* which echoes the Revelations of St. John the Divine. Oswald feels that he cannot evade death, which he visualizes as a beast that wishes to trample him into the ground with wide feet and to gore him with sharp horns. He then changes his imagery, saying that he has been summoned to a dance in which he must wear a wreath made of all his sins. This dance is, of course, a *Totentanz,* or *danse macabre,* the procession of skeletons and partially decomposed bodies that have left their tombs and are awaiting judgment. Oswald has often made good resolutions but has been unable to keep them; and now his heart is full of anxiety—not fear of death, but fear of what will come later, for he does not know where his soul will be on the next day (*und ist der tod die minst gezalt. O sel, wo bistu morgen?* 6/28). Even his children and relatives will be unable to help him on Judgment Day: they will inherit his wealth and leave him to go on his final journey alone. He knows that good works would have saved him; but, unfortunately, he has not performed many (6/36). Since he has loved the world more than God, his only hope lies in Mary's intercession.

As the previous song indicates, Oswald had little hope or desire to meet his Maker face to face, as Luther and his followers would do a century later; but he preferred to solicit divine favor through an intercessor. Whereas most of his contemporaries called upon many saints to intercede on their behalf, Oswald called only on the Virgin Mary, with the exception of one invocation to St. Catherine in the song *Ain anefangk* (1/9). To be sure, he built a chapel to his patron saint, Oswald, to thank him for rescuing him from the shipwreck; yet he never invokes him in his songs. Perhaps it is significant that he decorated the chapel with a picture of himself rather than with one of the saint. In his song *O wunnikliches paradis,* he swears by St. Peter, whom he should always praise in his songs (98/20); but these three exceptions are minimal. As the Mother of God, Mary could best persuade her Son to show mercy rather than justice on the Day of Wrath. Consequently, her cult was so popular that a stranger visiting Europe in Oswald's day and studying religious art and literature might well have concluded that Christianity was largely a matriarchal religion.

In addition to his numerous invocations of Mary in his various songs, Oswald also composed many songs for her or about her. German scholars call such songs *Marienlieder;* and we shall follow the custom, but with the reminder that *Marienlieder* do not constitute a genre but only a collectivity. In other words, the term is qualitatively no more meaningful than the term *Margaretenlieder* for the diverse songs written to or about Margaret. The individual *Marienlieder* fall into the genres or categories of *Loblied, Bittlied, Danklied, Passio,* and so on, the only thing they have in common being a common recipient or subject. This is illustrated in the case of one of Oswald's typical *Marienlieder,* a *Dienstlied* beginning *In Frankereich.*

Oswald begins *In Frankereich* with a list of sixteen kingdoms he has visited before finally finding a lady who will reward his services and be gracious even if he does not merit it. He then describes this beautiful lady with all the adjectives and epithets concocted by the minnesingers in their effort to ingratiate themselves with their patronesses. He next boasts of the four queens he has known, but only to give validity to his statement that his lady is more beautiful than any of these. Oswald repeats this technique of one-upmanship (or *Überbietungstopos,* to use Ernst Robert Curtius' term) in saying that Mary surpasses all the jewels of Paris, Venice, Bruges, Damascus, Tripolis, Genoa, Barcelona, and Montpellier. Besides her many physical charms, this beautiful lady can also sing expertly. Consequently, Oswald has determined to reject all other women and serve her alone. Two of the four queens referred to are the widowed Queen Margaret of Aragon and Queen Isabella of France, both of whom decorated Oswald's beard. The other two may have been the young queen of Aragon, Eleanora of Albuquerque, and the queen of Portugal, Philippina of Lancaster, or else Barbara, the wife of Sigismund, who was present at Constance.

Because the object of the above song was described in the clichés of courtly love service, many scholars, including two of the most recent ones, have assumed that it was addressed to Margaret. This is not possible, since Oswald refers to his lady's son (12/14) and also to her rose garden, in which she walks among the roses (12/33). However, the reference to Jesus and the rose garden are the only things that make this song a *Marienlied* rather than just a courtly secular song. The same two scholars also failed to recognize *Mich tröst ain adeliche mait* as a *Marienlied;* because it, too, praises Mary's physical charms in the standard terminology of secular love songs. There is no clear-cut evidence that this song is a *Marienlied,* since the *frouwen* or ladies of lofty love were also credited with chaste honor that could dampen all sinful lust with worthy salvation. Just as religious lyrics became worldly, so worldly ones often acquired religious overtones; and lofty love became a religious cult.

Mary is the subject of another courtly song, a song of praise and petition beginning *Wer ist, die da durchleuchtet.* Oswald begins each strophe with rhetorical questions, the first opening with "Who is it that shines brighter than the sun yet moistens our wilted wreath? Who is it that leads the dance and brings flowers to the beautiful May?" He then replies that it is a noble damsel, who chastely bore a Son who was her father and who will redeem us from hell. Since May Day had been a holy day of pagan fertility cults, the Church had wisely dedicated it to Mary in order to accommodate the popular festivities to Christian purpose.

The next strophe opens with the question of who can fully describe the maid, who is dearer than any other maid born on earth. Instead of answering the question, Oswald merely praises her rubylike brilliance and avows his certainty of winning her mercy. The third strophe asks who is the rose without thorns who will defend us on Judgment Day; and it implores the bright and true shield to break the devil's spear. The intricate pattern of internal rhymes in this song may reveal religious ardor, but it hardly betrays esthetic inspiration. Also rather forced is another *Loblied* and *Danklied* to Mary, namely *Wolauff, als das zu himel sei,* in which many clichés are crowded into three short strophes.

Oswald's mingling of erotic and religious imagery is even greater in his song *Es leucht durch graw,* which opens as a morning song and then changes abruptly into a May song in praise of Mary.

Es leucht durch graw die vein lasur	ma
durchsichtiklich gesprenget.	b
Blick durch die braw, rain creatur,	ma
mit aller zier gemenget.	b
Breislicher jan, dem niemand kan nach meim verstan	ccc
blasnieren neur ain füessel.	d
An tadels mail ist si so gail, wurd mir zu tail	eee
von ir ain freuntlich grüessel,	d
es wer mein swer mit ringer wag	nnf
volkomenlich gescheiden.	g
Von der man er lob singen mag	oof
ob allen schönen maiden.	g

The fine azure is shining through the gray in scattered transparent spots. Look through your brow, pure creation, and see all the adornment. The praiseworthy field (Mary), whom, in my opinion, no one can depict in the slightest, is so free of reproach and so joyful that all my sorrow would be completely ended, if I could but receive a little greeting from her. Of her one can sing honor and praises above all other beautiful maidens.

The song then continues as follows:

> The day is dawning joyfully bright, and all the meadows are resounding. In them birds are singing clearly, composing sweetly, and comfortingly plaiting strands of clear voice. The brightness of the flowers, the wreath of May, the splendor of the sun, and the high peaks of the firmament are serving the crown that immaculately bore us a Son for our joy. Where was there ever another bright and tender damsel who could give us more joy?
>
> Water, fire, earth, air, wind, treasures, the power of noble stones, and all wonders that can be found do not equal the pure maid who redeems me and comforts me daily. She is the highest in the cloister of my heart. Her tender person is immaculate. O pure rod (of Jesse), root of our joyful Easter, stand before the gates of dreadful punishment when my head sinks toward your fine red mouth (to receive the kiss of death?) and think of me kindly.

Here, despite the language and imagery derived from amorous lyrics, the song clearly revolves around the religious theme of Mary's redemption of sinners through the birth of her Son. The "power of noble stones" was taken very seriously in Oswald's day, as we see from the lapidaries that listed the various curative powers possessed by gems and other minerals.

The proximity of the sacred and the profane can be seen by comparing two of Oswald's May songs, *Des himels trone* and *Keuschlich geboren.* Although these have identical strophic patterns and are sung to the same melody, the one appears to be in honor of Margaret, while the other is dedicated to Mary and her Son. In both songs Oswald seems to have concentrated on achieving a strong rhythm, even at the cost of syntactical clarity. Mary is also honored in a Christmas hymn beginning *Freu dich, durchleuchtig junckfrau zart,* which was subsequently added to MS A but was omitted from MS B. Like its counterpart, the previously mentioned song *In Suria ain braiten hal,* it celebrates the birth of Jesus, whose praise occupies the majority of verses. In both songs Oswald gains credence for his story of the nativity by saying that he himself has been in Bethlehem (35/12, 126/5).

The longest of Oswald's *Marienlieder* is a *Compassio beatae virginis Mariae,* a song beginning *Hört zu* and describing Mary's anguish in witnessing Christ's suffering. Being based on the same Biblical stories, its plot is similar to that of the song *In oberland.*

In other words, it is actually a *Passio domini nostri* as seen by the eyewitness Mary, or, one might say, a *Mater dolorosa.*

Both MS A and MS B include a beautiful Latin hymn in praise of Mary, which begins *Ave, mater, o Maria.* This is composed in a stately octosyllabic rhythm popular in Latin hymnology since first introduced by St. Ambrose in the fourth century. Oswald's seventeen strophes consist of three mutually rhyming eight-syllable trochaic verses followed by a seven-syllable trochaic verse ending in the rhyme *O*, except for the last two strophes. As opposed to the *Korn* in the first fifteen strophes, the last two end in a *Waise* (orphan), or word that does not rhyme.

Ave, mater, o Maria	Hail, mother, oh Maria,
pietatis tota pia,	of devotion most devout,
sine te non erat via	without you there was no
deploranti seculo.	way for the weeping world.

This strophic form must once have been widespread; it was used, for example, in the hymn *Verbum bonum et suave,* which was well enough known to be parodied in a drinking song beginning:

Vinum bonum et suave,	Wine, both good and mellow,
bonis bonum, pravis prave,	good for the good and bad for
cunctis dulcis sapor, ave,	the depraved, sweet taste for
mundana letitia!	everyone, hail, worldly joy!

Although Oswald could speak Latin when occasion demanded (18/22), it is unlikely that his Latin was more fluent than his Hungarian, Moorish, or any of the other nine languages he claimed to know. At best he might have been able to ask a foreign priest how to find the nearest tavern. Surely he could not have composed such a splendid Latin hymn, not even a *cento* or "scissors and paste" conglomerate of verses gleaned from other songs. Probably he was not claiming authorship but merely included the lyrics in his anthology so they could be sung to the melody he had composed for them. His own talents are more evident in his German version *Ave, muotter, küniginne,* the first two strophes of which paraphrase the corresponding strophes of the Latin song, while the remaining two are more original.

Like most sexually wanton men, Oswald placed great value on

chastity in women; and, therefore, he was particularly awed by the virgin birth of Jesus. A comparison of Christianity with other religions would suggest that belief in the virgin birth had originally served to prove the divinity of Jesus, who was begotten of God rather than of man. By Oswald's day, however, the emphasis seems to have shifted from the divinity of Christ, which was by then no longer questioned, to the purity of Mary, who had never been soiled, defiled, or corrupted like other mothers. Some latter-day apologists for the medieval church claim that, since marriage was a sacrament, clergymen did not denigrate marital relations as necessarily vile, nasty, and sinful; yet many of them actually did so. Even Oswald seems to have shared this view in stressing the purity of his Lady, who is always referred to as a virgin (*maid*, 6/44; *rainer maid*, 35/6; *magt*, 109b/9; *magd vor und nach*, 114/6; *junckfrau*, 13/7). She is chaste (*keusch*, 13/18) and pure (*rain*, 12/67; *mäglichen rain*, 13/10). She bore Jesus chastely (*keuschlich*, 13/9, 114/80; *an mail*, 114/7) and remained uncorrupted or immaculate (*Ir leib so zart ist unverschart*, 34/31). Oswald marveled at Mary's purity because he, like many clerical celibates of his day, felt deep down in his heart that normal marital relations are sordid or sinful. It is to be noted that none of Oswald's frequently used epithets for Mary appears to allude to the Immaculate Conception, which was not yet dogma even if it had already been a popular belief in England and elsewhere two centuries earlier. Oswald also attests that Christ's birth not only caused Mary no blemish, but also no birth pains (*an we*, 38/40, 111/18, 126/4).

Whereas Oswald, like a true minnesinger, was faithful to his one heavenly mistress and never cultivated the other saints, he did compose two *Heiligenkalender*, or verse almanacs listing the various saints' days in sequence. One of these, *Menschlichen got*, was written to be sung, the other, *Genner beschnaid*, to be recited. Oswald called the first of these a *Cisiojanus*, which was the current term for such versified calendars. Composed for practical purposes, the two works have about as much literary merit as versified railroad timetables. They consist mainly of the names of the saints, with short comments about them that pad out the verses, facilitate the rhyme, and aid the memory. For anyone unfamiliar with the saints, many of these connective passages would be quite unintelligible. As Miriam Huebschmann has noted, neither calendar contains any recent saints, the latest being Bernard of Clairvaux and Thomas à Becket.[12] They omit even such well-known later saints as Thomas Aquinas, whom Oswald mentions elsewhere (111/49). This indicates that they must have followed a very old and unrevised source. Also, to judge from the provenience of many of the saints, it would seem that the source was compiled in the Archbishopric of Salzburg. It is difficult for most Protestants, and even for most modern Catholics, to realize how necessary it was in the Middle Ages to remember the feast days of the various saints. Nearly a century later, Magellan's sailors lost their leader and four of their five ships because, it was alleged, they celebrated the saints on the wrong days. Unfortunately for them, they knew nothing of the international date line.

It is apparent that Oswald's approach to religion was more emotional than intellectual; and only one of his songs goes into any theological detail. This is his confession song, *Mein sünd und schuld,* which is less a penitential lyric than a "mirror of sins" *(Sündenspiegel),* or model confession for others to follow.[13] It begins:

Mein sünd und schuld eu priester klag	a
an stat, der alle ding vermag.	a
Grob, lauter, schamrot, forchtlich das sag	a
durch andacht nasser ougen,	b
und hab ain fürsatz nimmer mer	c
mit vleiss zu sünden, wo ich ker.	c
Diemüetiklich mit willen, herr,	c
gib ich mich schuldig taugen.	b
An dem gelouben zweifel ich,	d
bei gottes namen swer ich vast.	e
Mein vatter und muotter erenreich	d
vertragen hab mit uberlast.	e

My sins and guilt I lament to you, priest, in place of Him who can do all things. I say it bluntly, clearly, blushing, and fearful with eyes wet with devotion. And I have resolved never to sin again intentionally, no matter where I turn. Humbly and voluntarily, Lord, I admit my sin in secret. I doubt in my faith. I often swear by God's name. My honorable father and mother I have grieved with a heavy load.

In this strophe, Oswald meets the chief requirements for confession: he regrets his sins, confesses them to a priest, and resolves not to commit them again. He then confesses to having violated the Ten Commandments, only four of which he covers in this strophe. Typical of Oswald is his odd quirk in saying that he has burdened his honorable father and mother instead of saying that he has failed to honor them. The next strophe continues with the Ten Commandments and then treats the seven mortal sins:

I am hasty to rob, steal, and kill; I am after people's life, honor, and property. I observe holy days and fasting reluctantly. False witness suits me well. I never have enough of gambling and other people's goods. I like sorcery, lying, disloyalty. I commit treachery and arson. My life is prideful. From greed I seldom rest. I am well versed in ridicule, anger, lechery, gluttony, and drinking late and early, lazy and envious as the ass and dog.

In the next strophe Oswald confesses to committing the "sins of others" *(peccata aliena)*, or actions by which one aids or abets other people to sin, and also to having neglected the six works of mercy. In addition, he admits having committed the four "atrocious sins," or the sins that "cry to heaven."

I command, advise, and commit sins. I make room for sins and favor them. I do not prevent the deed but participate without rebuking or reporting it. I have never acknowledged the naked nor averted thirst and hunger from the poor. To the sick, the dead, the captives, and the homeless I show no mercy. Innocent blood I have shed. Poor people I greatly oppress. I know the sin of Sodom. I pay only half of the wages earned.

In the next strophe, Oswald confesses to having sinned against the seven gifts of the Holy Ghost, the seven sacraments, and the eight beatitudes:

God's wisdom, understanding, knowledge, divine counsel, God's fortitude and ardor, fear of God, divine knowledge, divine goodness I never recognized. I scorn priests, commit adultery, disregard my baptism and confirmation. I receive God's body irreverently. I hate extreme unction, confession, and penance. Unresigned to poverty and evil, I rush through this temporal world as a poor sinner. Lacking mercy, I angrily hate God's justice despite His favors.

In the last two strophes, Oswald first confesses to having sinned with his five senses. He then tells his purpose for, and method of, composing his confession and asks the priest to give him proper penance:

My sight and hearing I use sinfully. My taste and scent, gourmandizing, my touch, going, thinking, I misuse without profit to the Lord. He who created heaven and earth and everything that dwells therein advised me, Wolkenstein, that through my confessional song I should teach many courtiers and many uncertain people who are erring in their skins, just as the geese are doing in Bohemia.

Therefore, with remorse and guilt, I have most sincerely acknowledged the ten commandments, the seven mortal sins, the whole swarm, the sins of others, the pure works of holy mercy, the gifts of the Holy Ghost, four crying sins, five senses. Oh Priest, give me grace! Through the holiness of the seven sacraments remit my sins! Take the eight blessednesses from me so that I will burn spiritually!

As we have seen, Oswald had previously described the sinful lives led by courtiers and had also polemicized against the "geese" in Bohemia. Whereas the theological contents of this song do not comfortably fit into the strophes, they do, with very minor exceptions, fit evenly into the quatrains of which the strophes are composed.

CHAPTER 4

An Appraisal

I *The Autobiographical Content of Oswald's Songs*

As the preceding chapters have indicated, Oswald seems to have related his own experience and expressed his own feelings and thoughts more often than any other medieval poet. Because the two major manuscripts of his songs were written during his lifetime, at his command, and probably under his supervision, we know that we have his words and melodies as he wished them and that we need not fear that time and transmission have corrupted them. Moreover, many of his songs are of a highly subjective nature; in fact, the first-person singular pronouns *ich, mir, mich,* and *mein* appear for a total of more than two thousand times.[1]

As previously mentioned, in the past scholars have accepted all of Oswald's songs at their face value and used them as historical sources for reconstructing his life. A reaction recently set in with the studies of Norbert Mayr and Ulrich Müller, who have questioned the previous use of his songs, particularly the use of his travel songs, as historical sources. Mayr first questioned the validity of Oswald's account of his early travels as narrated in his farewell to youth. Instead of running away from home, as earlier scholars had believed, Oswald probably left home under the tutelage of some experienced knight, possibly a kinsman, to whom his family entrusted him for training in the knightly arts. Mayr also questions whether little Oswald actually stayed away from Tyrol for a full decade, or whether he might not have returned home between various campaigns. Except for some minor points, such as these, which Oswald made many years after the event, Mayr did not question Oswald's honesty as much as he questioned the interpretations given his statements by modern scholars. Müller, on the other hand, questions Oswald's veracity, believing that there was a wide gulf between Oswald the man and Oswald the poet, that is to say, between the historical and the lyrical "I." [2]

The preceding interpretations of Oswald's songs indicate that we have little reason to discredit their factual content. Those few that can be compared with historical documents have proved to be true, so there is little justification for suspecting the others. If Oswald tells us that he has visited certain countries and met certain influential persons, we have no cause to question his honesty. Some scholars have doubted that he really traveled so extensively and have suggested that perhaps he was merely spinning a yarn, like the fabulous travelogues of the imaginary Englishman John Mandeville, whose memoirs enjoyed great popularity during Oswald's youth and were even translated by one of his kinsmen.

Wanderlust was a common attribute of idealized knights—for example, of the Knight in Chaucer's *Canterbury Tales*, who visited most of the same parts of the world as Oswald did. As we have seen in his song *Mich fragt ain ritter*, Oswald himself declared such travels to be suitable for a knight. This would suggest that he did not fabricate the accounts because they were the literary fashion, but rather that he actually undertook the travels in order to fulfill this accepted requirement of chivalry. As we have seen, in reciting his greatest worldly accomplishments in the song *O welt, o welt,* he put foreign travel first on his list, even before song, composition, knowledge, silver, and gold.

Oswald's journeys were all geographically feasible. There was a purpose underlying his trip to the Baltic countries, and it was quite logical to continue from there via the trade routes to the Black Sea. If Oswald really crossed the Black Sea in a merchant vessel, it would be only natural for it to land on the coasts of Georgia and Turkey, both of which then fronted on that water. Armenia was not far away, nor was Persia, which then dominated Mesopotamia and even Georgia (Ibera, or Ibernia as Oswald called it). Anyone in that part of the world would certainly wish to see Byzantium, which had been the easternmost bulwark of Christendom for a millennium. Scotland would not have been far out of the way for a ship sailing from the Baltic to Flanders; and Oswald also had good reason for going there after leaving Constance on a mission for Sigismund, who was most anxious to persuade the Scottish king to switch his allegiance from Pope Benedict. Since King John of Portugal was hiring soldiers from all over Europe for his campaign against Ceuta, it is possible that the ship carrying Oswald stopped at Ireland to take on troops, even though the Emerald Isle was then "beyond the pale" and perhaps the most out-of-the-way place that Oswald claims to have visited.

Oswald's words can also be trusted when he tells us of the very important people with whom he fraternized on his various journeys; for historical documents show that he was familiar with Emperor Sigismund, Rhinegrave Ludwig, and other high personages. Above all, we must remember that he sang his songs before close friends, who would have immediately become suspicious if he had named any lands or persons he could not have known at first hand. We should remember that, in the case of the only event he describes without having witnessed, to wit, the fracas at Ronciglione, he begins by admitting that his account is based on hearsay. His unfortunate extramarital escapade, in which he was thrashed by the four *Unger,* sounds too much like a farce to be taken seriously; and it is possible that Oswald called the narrator Hanns Maler in order to imply that the story did not really involve him, even if he told it in the first person for dramatic effect. If it was based on some personal experience, that experience may be reflected in the third mortal danger of his song *Wie vil ich sing und tichte,* in which he was captured, robbed, and severely beaten on his head (23/57–62). If the Hanns Maler episode was actually composed during Oswald's residence at Brixen, as I suspect, then he was not even married at the time. The old procuress in this song, who also appears as umpire in the debate between the burgher and the courtier, was a stock character in medieval literature, who is best represented by Trotaconventos in Juan Ruiz's *Book of Good Love* and by Celestina in Fernando de Rojas' *Calisto and Melebea.* I personally do not consider the Hanns Maler story to be a stylized version of the Sabina captivity, as Müller does.

Oswald may well have embroidered some of his tales in order to make them more amusing, but this does not undermine their basic credibility. A good example of such embellishment is found in the amusing anecdote of how he compelled Sigismund to give him an audience by excessively stoking the stove in the royal chamber; for this clever trick had not yet been introduced into the song when it was recorded in MS A. As Müller has demonstrated, the trick probably resulted from a "concretization" of the expression *jemandem einheizen* (to turn the heat on someone) and was added later even at the expense of a pure rhyme. In arguing that clerics twist justice even more than laymen do, Oswald asserts that he has witnessed such corruption in Rome. This may prove that he actually visited the Eternal City; but it is also possible that he was merely following a literary tradition popular since the goliardic poets, Walther, and others had attacked the corruption of the Papal Curia in that way.

Two anecdotes in the song of the seven mortal dangers also seem suspicious because they are too farcical. It is conceivable that Oswald once rode his horse down a cellar staircase, but it is highly improbable that he landed in a barrel of wine and that he had the presence of mind to offer a drink to the friends who came to his aid. Perhaps he nearly fell down the stairs, in which case he surely would have landed in a barrel of wine; but that would have made a far less entertaining story. In the other anecdote, Oswald saves his life in a shipwreck by clinging to a barrel—not just any barrel, but expressly a barrel of malmsey wine; and thus, as Müller has noted, he shares the experience of Stephano, who clings to a "butt of sack" in Act II, Sc. 2, of Shakespeare's *Tempest*. The earlier farewell to youth does not specify the content of Oswald's barrel, which may well have been flour, herrings, or some other foodstuff. That Oswald really clung to a barrel seems proved by a mural depicting the event in the Oswald Chapel, because it seems unlikely that the donor would have attributed a mendacious miracle to his patron saint. On the other hand, it is entirely possible that the mural was added after Oswald's death, and solely on the strength of his song. Obviously, the barrel in the mural did not reveal the nature of its contents.

We should not be too critical if Oswald occasionally distorted some minor facts for dramatic or rhetorical effect or for the sake of rhyme. When he says that he remained under water for over an hour, we know that the hyperbole is introduced for humorous effect. When he complains that, during the inflation at Überlingen, one egg cost sixteen hellers, we know that he is exaggerating, even if we question Ulrich von Richental's claim that eggs were always available at one heller each. When Oswald states that he has eaten kraut from the "Roman King's" platter (26/88), we are not to take this menu literally. In literature as well as in real life, kraut was the staple food for peasants, and

Oswald was only being facetious in attributing it to Sigismund's elegant table. The same is true of the kraut and porridge that was overly salted by the housemaid in *Wol auff, wir wellen slauffen* (84/36), for the noble tipsters would not have stooped to eat such lowly fare. Dietary satire was, and long remained, a favorite element of upper-class humor.[3]

When Oswald says that he was bound in prison with five irons, five may have been an arbitrary number. Possibly he first had six, later four or three. Five would have had symbolic significance, being the number of Christ's wounds. When he says that he was bound in prison with chains and ropes (*mit eisen und mit sail,* 1/50), it is evident that he chose the latter word only to rhyme with *gail,* since he has said elsewhere that he was fettered with forged iron (*ingesmitt,* 2/68). Ropes are useful in binding a freshly captured man, as Oswald was when betrayed by Sabina (*mit sailen zuo gesnuoret,* 23/75), but they would not do for a long imprisonment. Although most critics refer to Oswald's torture *(Folter),* we should note that he himself never mentions it. To be sure, he often uses the word *qual,* but that refers to his spiritual anguish and physical distress at being captured and chained so painfully. He never once implies that torture was applied to force him to yield to his captors' demands. The leg-iron that chafed his shin must have been very painful; but its purpose was to restrain him, not to torture him. If such a self-centered, self-commiserating, and wrongfully punished man had been subjected to torture, he would surely have complained of it. Some scholars contend that Oswald was subjected to a common type of torture in which the victim's hands are tied behind his back and then he is hoisted up by them so that his arms are wrenched out of their shoulder sockets. This was surely not Oswald's fate, or else he would have been unable to use, much less to hug, his crutch during the *Fasching* celebration.

Once we make allowance for amusing elaboration or exaggeration for effect, we have little right to disbelieve Oswald's factual statements; but we are justified in questioning his statements about his subjective motivation. As we have noted, it was customary in his day to attribute deeds of daring to the service of a lady; and we have every reason to suspect that Oswald would have made his pilgrimage to the Holy Land even if he had not known Sabina. Nevertheless, given the training he received, he may very well have been sincere in thinking that he went there in her service.

Oswald's paradoxical nature is nowhere better revealed than in his attitude toward love. Sometimes he is the languishing lover of minnesong tradition, who serves selflessly in hope of a mere acknowledgment. At other times, he is the gay seducer, for whom a woman merely offers pleasant physical gratification. Sometimes he praises women for the purity of their character, at other times for the voluptuousness of their bodies. But the carnal desires expressed in his *Ain tunckle farb* are far more convincing than all his protestations of romantic love.

The same might be said about Oswald's attitude toward religion. Religion meant something to him in prison when he was in fear of death, but sometimes it appears to have served as an acceptable theme for literary composition that would win human approbation as well as divine favor. Like most people of his age, and many of ours, Oswald lacked introspection and was probably unaware of his contradictory attitudes toward worldly and otherworldly values. Or one might say that he was consistent: when he served God he denied the world completely, and when he served the world he did so without restraint.

These apparent discrepancies can be explained by the German adage *Die Rolle prägt den Kopf,* which means that the role in a drama decides how the character will behave. Applied to Oswald, the adage could be restated: *Die Gattung prägt den Kopf,* or the genre determines the poet's outlook. When Oswald sings a *Minnelied,* he is a languishing lover. When he sings a pastourelle, he is a gay seducer. When he sings a summer song, he is a boisterous dancer; and, when he sings an *Alterslied,* he is an old man disillusioned by the foibles of the world.

Such a theory would seem to discredit all autobiographic content in Oswald's songs and to imply that he never revealed his true feelings. But that is not the case: he was free to choose whatever genre he wished, and he naturally chose the one most compatible with the mood he was currently in. While Oswald was in prison, he was still a young man; yet fear and despair put him in a frame of mind that could best be expressed by means of an *Alterslied* or a memento mori. As a man of substance, he could be much more honest than any professional poet like Walther, who might have to accept a commission to compose a song in conflict with his current sentiments, a song which would require him to weep when he would rather laugh, or laugh when he would rather weep. As previously noted, two of Oswald's ostensibly religious prison songs may have had a diplomatic aim; and his Hauenstein song may also have had an ulterior purpose. But these are exceptional, for the great majority of Oswald's songs seem to express his immediate and unhampered feelings. Some of his songs, such as his Greifenstein song, his drinking songs, and his outcries from the dungeon, reveal little difference between the lyrical and the historical "I."

Because Oswald was financially independent of his music, one might ask why he devoted so much of his leisure to it. Obviously he derived esthetic enjoyment and emotional release from it and had a natural urge to sing, or, as he put it, *Mein singen mag ich nicht gelan* (I cannot stop singing, 116/18). Having only one eye, he developed his sense of hearing far beyond that of most men; and his songs constantly reveal how receptive he was to beautiful sounds and how repelled he was by ugly ones. Music, singing, and bird songs could put him into ecstasy, whereas the crying of children, the screeching of peacocks, the braying of donkeys, and the rushing of a stream could shatter his equanimity. Subjective factors naturally played a role, too; for the unwelcome domestic noises just mentioned were surely no more raucous than the blowing of horns and the yelping of hounds in his hunting song, which were balm for his ears.

In his farewell to youth, Oswald boasts that he learned to play fiddles, trumpets, drums, and fifes and that he had spent his life in composing and singing all sorts of things (18/24, 98). Subsequently, he never failed to mention the joyful singing *(singen und schallen)* that occurred on his visits to Munich, Augsburg, and other cities. For him, singing was such a noble art that he attributed a good voice to Maria—an idea perhaps suggested by the many pictures depicting her holding a psalter. He praises his own tenor voice by contrasting it with the croaking voice of his imaginary old age (5/18); and, like Walther, he proudly reports that he was called the nightingale (81/26).

But Oswald had more than an esthetic need for singing. He sang in order to win attention and approval. Because he had lost an eye, he felt great insecurity with other people, especially in the presence of women, as will be seen from the fact that all his references to his missing eye are found in songs to or about women. This diffidence gave him an unusually strong *Geltungsbedürfnis,* or need for recognition. It explains, on the one hand, his ruthless zeal in aggrandizing his property and thus raising his status; on the other hand, it explains his great need for being the center of attention. When, in his Heidelberg song, he reminisces about the singing in Munich and Augsburg, we can assume that he not only participated but also scintillated. His greatest pride was having sung before queens, and one song suggests that he sang for Queen Margaret prior to being honored by her (12/37–42). He sings his paraphrase of Freidank's *Bescheidenheit* because people would soon forget him if he were to stop singing (117/1).

We have seen that Oswald's craving for attention was so strong that he was willing to play the fool in order to win it. The Perpignan song should have been a story of "The King and I"; but Oswald was able to make it "I and the king," thereby deflecting much of the attention from Sigismund, the terminator of the Great Schism, to Wolkenstein, the family fool. Oswald certainly gained little admiration for his sorry role as laughingstock for the Augsburg dancing girls, but his amusing account of it must have brought him much applause from his audience. It is possible, of course, that, like Hamlet, he acted the buffoon in order to allay suspicion while he was engaged in his political intrigues.

It will be noted that the fictitious hero of Oswald's songs is usually the passive victim, whereas the historical Oswald was a man of untiring energy and activity. It is, therefore, possible that the passive life of the fictitious "I" served as an emotional release for the overly active and ambitious historical "I"; because, as wish-fulfilment, authors often create alter egos contrary to themselves. This is illustrated, for example, by many irresponsible, casual, art-loving ne'er-do-wells in nineteenth-century German literature who were produced by diligent, hard-working, and duty-conscious public servants. The discrepancy between Oswald's lyrical and historical "I" is most striking in his *Alterslieder* (some of which, we have noticed, were produced in his best years!). Despite the world-weary disillusionment expressed in such songs, Oswald remained vigorous and ruthless in his personal affairs almost to the day of his death.

II *Oswald's Art*

Oswald is scarcely mentioned, and then often disparagingly, in most early histories of German literature, whose authors had more and better things to say about Walther and his Hohenstaufen contemporaries. This was because they understood neither Oswald's language nor his poetic intentions. Whenever they could not understand his meaning, they assumed that he was talking nonsense or using dialect or nonce-words. In the last two decades, many of Oswald's obscure songs have been elucidated; and we can now conclude that, in cases where we cannot understand one of his verses, the fault may lie in our ignorance of his vocabulary rather than in his failure to express himself correctly. Above all, we have learned to judge him by the standards of his day, not by those of our day or even by those of the Hohenstaufen period. His deviations from the threadbare norms of minnesong should not be judged as a decline or failure, but rather as a healthy breakthrough to a more expressive art.

Oswald's apparent shortcomings should be attributed less to him personally than to the taste of his age; for we cannot blame a poet who excels in the art demanded of him by his most discriminating contemporaries. Critics object to Oswald's choice of highly intricate rhyme schemes, like those of the mastersingers, which sometimes cost him more effort than he spent in formulating his thoughts. But this was the fault of his age, and instead of blaming him we would do better to marvel at his technical dexterity in resolving the exigencies of his ill-chosen rhyme patterns.

When first reading Oswald's poems, the reader will object to his use of genitive rhymes, that is to say, to his adding a convenient rhyme word to the intended word, which is then put in the genitive. For example, because "honor" does not rhyme easily, it can be replaced with "honor's name" to rhyme with "fame" or by "honor's crown" to rhyme with "renown." In some cases, the genitive rhymes actually enhance the meaning, as in the case with *der sunne glanz*, which stresses the sun's brilliance, or *der sunden gall*, which implies that sin brings bitter sorrow, or *des herzen grund*, which suggests that the emotion involved is borne in the very depth of the heart. Sometimes the genitive expression is neutral, neither adding nor detracting from the meaning, as in the case of *der erden phat*, the path of the world, *der helle hal,* the hall of hell, or *der eren geude,* the enjoyment of honor, all of which means neither more nor less than earth, hell, and honor. Sometimes the genitive expression definitely detracts from the intended meaning, as is the case with *des heilgen gaistes stein,* the stone of the Holy Ghost, *der helle vas,* the receptacle of hell, or *des leibes sal,* the hall of the body. These genitive periphrases are particularly annoying, to us, when they are excessively used as, for example, in the song *Es seusst dort her von orient,* where there are six of them in sixteen lines (20/50–65). But we should remember that Oswald was probably racking his brain to devise these and thus impress his audience.

Whenever we are offended with what appears to be a forced rhyme, we should recall that the trouble may lie in our ignorance rather than in Oswald's inability. This has recently been shown, for example, in the case of Oswald's sarcastic song *Solt ich von sorgen werden greis,* in which he says that, should he ever grow gray with worry and become clever and wise only after the damage is done, it will be due to *meines buolen breis* (59/3). Assuming that *breis* meant "praise," critics have interpreted this as a figure of speech for "my praiseworthy sweetheart" and thus a rather uninspired genitive rhyme. But now Lambertus Okken has recently discovered that *breis* also meant "cuff-links" and refers in this passage to the manacles Sabina made Oswald wear. This fits perfectly with the following verses, which contrast the golden bracelet Oswald used to wear in Sabina's honor with the three-inch-wide iron bands he now wears at her command.

We have no more right to censure Oswald's genitive rhymes than to censure the Victorian poets' "sight rhymes," which cannot be justified on any esthetic grounds whatever. Surely two differently sounding words should not "rhyme" merely because our archaic English orthography happens to represent them with similar graphemes. To realize the absurdity of this practice, one should recite his favorite verses from his uncritical childhood and force them to rhyme, for example: "By the rude bridge that arched the flood, There the embattled farmers stud." Because such rhymes were so prevalent in the nineteenth century, it is a moot question whether, between the dark and the daylight, the night is beginning to lour or to get lower. In contrast to sight rhymes, Oswald's genitive rhymes never offend the ear and seldom the mind, especially when they are sung. One learned scholar has classified many of Oswald's impure rhymes as sight rhymes *(Augenreime)*, but I consider this to be entirely wrong. Oswald was singing to appeal to his hearers' ears, not their eyes. Besides, most members of his audience were illiterate; and illiterate people would be unimpressed, even if they knew that two impure rhymes would happen to look alike if written down at the same time by the same scribe.

In view of the intricate rhyme schemes he affected, Oswald's rhymes tend to be as pure as could be expected. There was no standard pronunciation in his day and no way for him to know which rhymes were acceptable away from home until he saw the reaction of his audience. The rhymes that came to him most naturally were those of his native Tyrolian dialect, since both his parents and nearly all his friends and kinsmen were deeply rooted in that area. When traveling in the great world, he naturally tried to conform as best he could; and, in view of his very extensive travels, he could, no doubt, speak a relatively dialect-free "common German." As king of Hungary, Sigismund may have had an East German pronunciation; and Rhinegrave Ludwig may have revealed his Upper Rhineland dialect. However, the higher nobility, being often of interregional or even international parentage, probably betrayed their local dialects much less noticeably than did the lesser and rural nobility. The imperial court, which was staffed by people from all German-speaking territories, must have had a somewhat standardized pronunciation, to which everyone, especially singers, would try to conform.

It is evident that Oswald allowed himself the use of Bavarian rhymes in his rustic songs. Such rhymes would be most fitting in the speech of the peasant protagonists and also for describing rustic life, especially if the intended audience itself spoke the Bavarian dialect. In songs sung to outlanders like Sigismund and Ludwig, Oswald seems to have tried to avoid such vulgarisms. The apparent discrepancies in his rhymes can be attributed chiefly to his adoption of "literary rhymes," or rhymes that he accepted along with his literary sources. Finding a suitable ready-made rhyme pair in his source, Oswald may well have retained it even if it differed from his normal usage. "Literary rhymes" are, of course, simply dialect rhymes seen from the outsider's point of view. These are still permitted in German verse. A North German would never rhyme *schneit* and *erfreut* in speech, but he accepts them as rhymes in singing about the *Tannenbaum* that gives him joy even in "winter" when it "snows," because those two words rhymed in the composer's Bavarian dialect, and incidentally in Oswald's too. As a Rhinelander, Heinrich Heine would never have rhymed *Weh* with *Höh* in speech, yet he felt free to do so in his *Lorelei* because Swabian poets had long been permitted to do so. When we thank the Gracious Giver of all *good* for our rest and *food,* we are not perpetrating a sight rhyme, but are merely perpetuating a literary rhyme which was perfectly pure for the Scots poet who composed this little blessing. Oswald's rhymes will remain a mystery unless some well-trained structural linguist makes a complete analysis of the phonology of the Eisack Valley dialect in Oswald's day.

III *Oswald's Originality*

It has been shown that several of Oswald's songs, particularly among his least attractive ones, were based on literary models: his aphoristic didactic song *Wer hie umb diser welde lust* is a reworking of a portion of Freidank's *Bescheidenheit,* his temperance appeal *Und swig ich nu* is a paraphrase of a Latin work, and his ornithological medley *Der mai mit lieber zal* was based on an older work. However, even if more analogues and possible sources should be discovered, Oswald will still be judged as an exceptionally original poet, especially for the fifteenth century, which had other ideas about literary creation than ours.

In the Middle Ages, only God was a creator: at best, man could re-create. Therefore, it made little difference whether a poet re-created from personal experience and observation or from literary sources, except that the latter method was frequently felt to be more honest and authoritative, with the result that poets often claimed written sources even for products of their own fantasy. Oswald's exceptional originality may result less from a desire to be original than from an uncontrollable impulse to express his thoughts and feelings immediately, without waiting to find traditional channels for doing so. Like Chaucer's Wife of Bath, Oswald found experience to be enough and had little need of "auctoritee."

Regardless of his sources, Oswald put his personal stamp on everything he composed. If his Überlingen song had been omitted from the Wolkenstein manuscripts and were only now to come to light anonymously, any Oswald enthusiast would immediately recognize his handiwork. That would also hold true of the Augsburg and Constance songs, to say nothing of his Ronciglione kermess, his diatribe against wicked women, and a host of other songs. His authorship would be betrayed not only by a number of individual and personal stylistic touches, but also by his intensity of feeling and by the directness of its expression.

It is generally assumed that Oswald read his literary sources; but I contend that he most often heard them, usually sung rather than spoken. Because literature is now written, we tend to forget that oral traditions were millennia older than writing and even survived the invention of writing. Whereas the English word "literature" is derived from the word *litterae* (letters), the German word *Dichtung* is derived from *dicere* (to speak); and as late as Oswald's day poetic composition was usually a matter of dictation. It is often stated that Oswald corrected his two manuscripts with his own hand; but I am not at all convinced that he could write, or even that he ever read. Reading and writing were menial tasks which a gentleman could delegate to an underling; and there was no more incentive then for a gentleman to write than there is for an admiral or corporation president to do his own typing. The illustrations of the Great Heidelberg Manuscript show the minnesingers dictating to their scribes (who are drawn smaller to show their lesser importance), and Ulrich of Lichtenstein remained on tenterhooks for weeks while waiting for his own trusted scribe to return and read him a letter from his lady. There is no evidence that literacy greatly increased among the landed nobility during the intervening two centuries, even if it was spreading for business reasons among the new middle class.

Oswald was the social peer of the canons of the cathedral at Brixen, whom he supported against their bishop, and there is no reason to suppose that they were less educated than he was; yet not one of the canons there during his childhood could sign his name. There are numerous letters from Oswald, including casual and personal ones to his wife; but none of them seems to have been written in his own handwriting, which cannot even be identified. It will be noted that he makes only two literary references in all his songs, those to Petrarch and Aquinas, and these suggest that he had *not* read their works. In order to be convinced of Oswald's illiteracy, one should contrast him with the contemporary burghers Geoffrey Chaucer and Henry Wittenwiler, who correctly cited scores of learned Latin and French authorities. On the few occasions Oswald followed written sources, such as in his reworking of Freidank's *Bescheidenheit,* the scribe could have read out the original couplets, which Oswald usually padded out into quatrains for the sake of rhyme. The same would have held of any Latin or Old French source. The scribe rendered it into German, which Oswald then versified. Oswald was probably speaking ingenuously when he said that people read and tell us much about past ages (*Man list und sagt uns vil von alden jaren,* 10/31). If we accept Oswald's word that he spent the second decade of his life in travel and hardship, he would have had very little time for any formal education, for the perimeters of the known world were not conducive to applied study.

Oswald died only a few years before Gutenberg perfected his use of movable type, that is to say, just before Europe changed from an auditory to a visual culture. Some people might doubt that Oswald could have created such complicated strophic structures without putting them down on paper, but that is only because they themselves have developed their sense of sight at the expense of that of sound. Oswald was working primarily with music and only secondarily with lyrics; and the demands of the tune prevailed over the words, which could be altered, rearranged, or replaced to meet the metrical requirements.

Like the Serbo-Croatian folk singers studied by Milman Parry and Albert B. Lord, in fact like folk singers in general and including many of our popular radio and television entertainers, Oswald surely started his career by learning and performing other people's songs. First he learned their techniques and amassed a stockpile of musical and poetic phrases; then he started composing on his own, probably in close imitation of his models. Some of his love lyrics would seem to date from this early period. The earliest song we can definitely date is his pilgrimage song of about 1409, when he was some thirty-two years of age. It is very possible that he, like Hugo of Montfort, employed a musically trained scribe, who would not only have notated his songs but also have taught him some theory and the kind of musical terminology that he flaunts in his song *In Frankereich* (12/49–52).

That Oswald's interests were auditory rather than visual is confirmed by his amazing mastery of the language, which he manipulated with incredible skill. His vocabulary is exceedingly rich in nouns connoting sounds and in adjectives distinguishing their qualities. Many of his songs gain their impact more from their acoustic effect than from their lexical meaning; and he excels in onomatopoeia—for example, in the bird songs in his *Der mai mit lieber zal.* It is regrettable that, instead of enjoying the irresistible rhythms of his dance refrains, some critics have squandered their time in trying to decipher them. Oswald's long lists of geographical names not only impressed his hearers with his exploits but also furnished auditory enjoyment. In addition to exhibiting elaborate rhyme schemes, his songs also juxtapose rhyme pairs that harmonize together: for example, in *Ain mensch von achzehen jaren kluog,* the rhyme of *kluog–genuog* harmonizes with that of *ruo–fruo–zuo,* and that of *lant–bekannt* harmonizes with that of *gedanckh–dranck–vanck.* Instead of pure rhymes, Oswald sometimes uses assonances, or rhymes in which the vowels are similar but the following consonants are not. But even here, consciously or otherwise, he rigidly limits himself to assonances in which the consonants are homorganic. That is to say that a voiced stop like *b* can rhyme with a voiced stop like *d* or *g,* but not with a voiceless stop like *t* or *k.* Oswald is most lavish in his use of alliteration, as William T. H. Jackson has amply demonstrated.

Critics have sometimes complained of the formlessness of Oswald's longer works, in which the episodes often follow each other in no recognizably logical or chronological order. For example, in his farewell to youth, he recalls his audience with Queen Margaret in the third strophe, whereas the previous Palestine pilgrimage is relegated to the fourth. In his Perpignan song, he relates his and Sigismund's departures from Paris before he tells about the promotion of Amadeus to the rank of duke, although this ceremony had occurred much earlier. But to criticize such apparent oversights is to misunderstand Oswald, who never looked at the world with detachment but was a prisoner in it. He gave his impressions directly, that is to say, in the order in which he recollected them. His impressions and episodes do not follow in any causal sequence, what binds them is the fact that they are experienced by the same subject. Oswald could have rectified such disorder while editing MS B if he had thought it desirable, but obviously he did not. Sometimes the opening proverb is supposed to give a central idea to the various episodes, but even then they are not subordinated to it. The disjointedness of some of Oswald's longer songs suggests the *Teilperspektiv* of many paintings of his and the following century, for example, Pieter Breughel the Elder's complex scenes, which contain numerous details capable of standing alone and scarcely integrated into an overall pattern.

Herbert Löwenstein maintains that Oswald tended to use a common melody for songs of similar mood; and as evidence he shows that the melody used for the songs of the first captivity was also used for four songs in which Oswald is abused by women, namely, in two songs about Sabina: *Mein buol laisst mir gesellschaft zwar* and *Solt ich von sorgen werden greis*, and in two songs about the girls in Augsburg and Constance: *Wol auf, gesellen* and *Der seines laids ergeczt well sein.* To be sure, all these songs are complaints; yet they certainly differ in mood, since some are serious and some are only pseudoserious. In like manner, a single melody is used for both the serious (albeit also amusing) Hauenstein song and the entirely jocular Überlingen song. In most cases there seems to be no correlation whatever between the moods of the songs sung to a common melody. Typical is the discrepancy between the erotic fantasy *Ain tunckle farb* and the two religious songs *Es leucht durch graw* and *In Suria ain braiten hal.* We have seen that no distinction was made between sacred and profane music.

Although a prisoner in the world, Oswald was concerned only with that part of it immediately affecting him. The crucial battle of Agincourt, in which the English destroyed the flower of French chivalry, occurred while Oswald was in France, yet he did not deign to mention it in his Perpignan song because it did not concern him and he did not experience it personally. Except in a few of his later didactic songs, he never sang as a representative of mankind, but only as a solitary individual; and, except in his religious songs, he was more concerned with the fleeting moment than with permanence. Despite his vital energy, he usually presents himself playing a passive role. Almost the only exception is his active role in his Greifenstein song, but even there he is only the second of three participants.

Perhaps the most enjoyable feature of Oswald's songs is his unbridled humor. Whereas his dietary and other social satire is largely lost on us today, we can still laugh at his self-ridicule in presenting himself as the laughingstock for the court or as the victim of rough treatment. An unexpected twist can occur at any time. During his extramarital excursion he lies down next to his sweetheart in expectation of amorous pleasure, but all he receives is a beating from four irate men. When he lures the berry picker into his bird blind, we are not surprised that he seduces her; but we are surprised that she then becomes the aggressor and puts him to shame. Very unexpected, and thoroughly Oswaldian, is the addition of his own name as the last but not the least of the world's greatest dupes of love.

Oswald's puns are very clever, for example when he says that the host is modest *(beschaiden)* and can cut *(schaiden)* the gold from one's purse. His play on names like Hecht, Bösaier, de Luna, and Dulce are still amusing, once explained. The same hold true of his wry humor in making absurd statements with a straight face but tongue in cheek, as when he says that he brought two and a half horses with him from Narbonne (19/128) or that a deaf mute had told him that the cowhide that served him as a bed had come from a cow named Mumme (19/71). Purposely twisted logic is seen when, after praising a woman's beautiful pear-shaped breasts, he reflects that, were he a little baby, yet wise and old, and were he permitted to suck one of them, he would never grow gray. Obviously, at that age his interest in her bosom would be nutritional rather than erotic, and he would be in no immediate danger of growing gray. There is also absurdity in his exaggerations, such as that he had remained underwater for an hour or that Sigismund had given him more gold than three men could carry. Oswald must have seen the inappropriateness and absurdity of shaming his lady into showing him mercy by citing the proverb that it is better to die young than to live in shame for two hundred years.

Most characteristic of Oswald's humor is his practice of arousing great expectations, which then turn out contrary to what is expected. Müller uses the terms *Ankündigung* and *Ausführung* to describe this procedure in Oswald's farewell to youth, when the little boy sets out to see the world but only experiences hardship, and later when he sets out as a knight-errant in love service but ends up as a foundered merchant. Similar surprise is caused in the Hauenstein song when Oswald tells us that he had many kinds of entertainment, such as donkey's singing and peacock's screaming (44/61). Likewise, in ironically praising the food in Überlingen, he says that the pigs there are fat; but then he adds that they are fattened on chaff. This immediately negates his assertion and twists it into its opposite. One would expect him to say that they are fattened on mash; therefore, if they are "fattened" on chaff, they must really be very thin. And, to appreciate this humor, we must remember that fat pork was then more desirable than lean.

The Überlingen song also furnishes many examples of one of Oswald's favorite humorous devices, which we might call the *ungleicher Vergleich*, or dissimilar simile. He says that the wine there is very sweet, like sloeberry drink; in other words, it is very bitter. It brings us joy just as the sack brings joy to the donkey, which suggests the beatified joy on the donkey's face when he sees the miller approaching with the heavy sack. The serving girl has little breasts, just like bats; her feet are as slender as shields; her little legs are turned as well as a thick beech log; her hands and arms are as white as a crow.

Perhaps the most refreshing feature of Oswald's songs is their vigor and vitality. As a general rule of thumb, most modern lyric poets have been effete. The sensitivity required for producing lyric verse is most often found in social and physical misfits, in the physically weak, the mentally unbalanced, the emotionally disturbed, and the sexually uncertain—in troubled souls whose poems serve as an escape from a world with which they cannot cope. Of course, there are enough wholesome exceptions to prove the rule, but they are greatly outnumbered by less virile natures.

Oswald was a rugged individual, a man as much at home in the barracks or brothel as at court or cloister. Totally lacking in introspection and reserve, he frankly revealed his joys, hopes, fears, and anxieties, which he expressed in lyrics that are part and parcel of the melodies that sustain them. Now that, by a quirk of history, many attitudes and outlooks of his apocalyptic era are beginning to reappear in our own topsy-turvy world, his recent popularity is sure to continue and even to increase. In the nineteenth century, interest in Oswald was largely a matter of local patriotism, research being conducted almost only in Tyrol and other parts of Austria. The early twentieth century saw his fame spread to other German-speaking areas, and now at last he has become a world poet, as is shown by scholarly studies recently devoted to him in Italy, the United Kingdom, the United States, Australia, the Netherlands, Japan, and elsewhere. It is hoped that this study will encourage still more people to become better acquainted with this fascinating and all-too-human artist.

Notes and References

Preface

1. All unannotated titles in the text appear in the bibliography.
2. *Das Liederbuch der Klara Hätzlerin,* ed. Carl Haltaus. (Quedlinburg and Leipzig, 1840). Reprint by Hanns Fischer (Berlin, 1966).
3. Beda Weber, *Oswald von Wolkenstein und Friedrich mit der leeren Tasche.* (Innsbruck, 1850).

Chapter One

1. George F. Jones, *Walther von der Vogelweide.* (New York: Twayne Publishers, 1968).
2. This is confirmed in *O welt, o welt,* another song composed in captivity, in which Oswald says that he has enjoyed her love for twelve and a half years (9/11).
3. The expression *ins Tal Josaphat laden* (to invite to the Valley of Josaphat) was an idiom meaning "to cause someone injury." If this was Oswald's meaning here, then the song does not necessarily concern a Palestinian pilgrimage.
4. I take *wild* to be a Bavarian spelling for *bild* (Cf. *berche* for *wercke*). However, even if *wild* does mean "game," a concept better suited to the image of the snare *(latz),* the context still makes it evident that the word refers to her womanly reputation.
5. Banta, Frank. "Dimensions." For full title, see bibliography.
6. See Selected Bibliography, Primary Sources.

Chapter Two

1. *Ulrich von Richentals Konstanzer Chronik,* ed. M. R. Buck. Stuttgart, 1882 (Bibliothek des Literarischen Vereins Stuttgart, 158); Thomas Prischuch, *Des conzilis Grundfeste,* in: *Die historischen Volkslieder der Deutschen,* ed. R. von Liliencron (Leipzig, 1865), I, p. 228, no. 50. See also nos. 51–54.
2. Mayr (*Reiselieder,* p. 76) denies that this Fritz was Friedrich von Hohenzollern, who accompanied Sigismund only as far as Bern; but he produces no evidence that Friedrich did not follow later.

3. Reproduced in *Deutsche Literatur im späten Mittelalter 1250–1450*, ed. F.-W. Wentzlaff-Eggebert. (Hamburg: Rowohlt, 1971), no. 79. This letter was written on the Friday after Corpus Christi, 1445.

4. MS B reads *Crafft not* (19/201), which is obviously a scribal error for *ehaft not*, as it appears in MS A. This denoted a situation legally justifying one's absence.

5. This must have been a drinking song in honor of a cooked goose, like the Latin song *Olim lacus colueram* (*Carmina Burana*, ed. Hilka-Schumann, no. 130), the complaint of a roasted swan, which has been translated in *Medieval Song*, tr. James J. Wilhelm. (New York: E. P. Dutton, 1971), no. 34.

6. Oswald literally says that she rode him in courtly fashion (*hoflichen si in rait*, 3/34). He is alluding to a popular medieval anecdote that, in order to win the favors of Thaïs, Alexander the Great's mistress, Aristotle promised to carry her on his back like a horse and was humiliated when she arranged for the entire court to witness the spectacle, thus proving that age is no protection against folly (*Das Alter schützt vor Torheit nicht;* There's no fool like an old fool).

7. Petzsch, *Melodietypenveränderung*. . . .

8. Petzsch (*ibid.*, p. 496) has added the word *we*, which appears in neither MS A nor MS B. Although opposed in principle to emendations, I think that this one is justified.

9. This song is somewhat more fully and frankly discussed in George F. Jones, "Ain tunckle farb," *Zeitschrift für deutsche Philologie* XC(1971), *Sonderheft*, 142–153.

10. Ulrich Müller, "Ovid 'Amores'–alba–tageliet," *Sonderdruck der Vierteljahrsschrift für Literaturwissenschaft und Geistesgeschichte* XLV (1971), 451–80.

11. See note 2, above.

12. One of Walter Scott's earliest literary endeavors was a translation of Goethe's drama *Götz von Berlichingen*, which contains a vivid scene of the *Feme*. Many years later he reused this scene in grinding out a potboiler, *Anna of Geierstein*. Like all of Scott's novels, this one was immensely popular in the Antebellum South, which welcomed a medieval mystique to justify slavery and class discrimination. During Reconstruction, some students at Sewanee College remembered this scene and saw that its rituals and costumes well suited the vigilante organization they were planning.

Chapter Three

1. Mayr (p. 101) believes that the joys experienced at Nuremberg and Constance refer to Oswald's sojourn there in 1431, in which case the song *Von trauren möcht ich werden taub* would have to have been composed later.

2. See note 3 to Chapter II.

3. Both songs were added to MS A at the same time or after they were put in MS B. The scribal differences are minimal, being almost entirely limited to orthography. In one case, MS A has *keulen* (116/17) where MS B has the more logical *beulen* (105/17). Perhaps the scribe of MS A was misled by the *keulen* in v. 13.

4. Mayr (p. 109) believes that the *hechtigin* refers to Gülcher (Peter Kalde), who was from Jülich and therefore spoke Low German; but the liver referred to surely belonged to Hecht.

5. The two last verses are enigmatic. Although the words *der van* appear in both MS A and MS B, they are probably an error. The scribe of MS C changed them to *davon*. My solution is based on similar suggestions by Lambertus Okken, Ulrich Müller, and Jere Fleck.

7. See Helmut Rehder, "Planetenkinder: Some Problems of Character Portrayal in Literature." *The Graduate Journal* VIII (1968), 69–97.

8. See Gerhard Eis, *Mittelalterliche Fachliteratur*. Stuttgart: Metzler, 1962; Gerhard Eis, *Forschungen zur Fachprosa*. Bern: Francke Verlag, 1971; *Fachliteratur des Mittelalters, Festschrift für Gerhard Eis*, ed. Gundolf Keil, et al. Stuttgart: Metzler, 1968.

Chapter Four

1. A preliminary computer count found 2287 uses of the first person singular pronoun in MS B alone.

2. See Ulrich Müller, "Lügende Dichter . . ."

3. See George F. Jones, "The Function of Food in Medieval Literature," *Speculum* xxv (1960), 78–86.

Selected Bibliography

PRIMARY SOURCES

1. Editions:

Oswald von Wolkenstein: Geistliche und weltliche Lieder, ein- und mehrstimmig, ed. Josef Schatz. Vienna 1902 (*Denkmäler der Tonkunst in Österreich,* 18); Sec. ed.

Die Lieder Oswalds von Wolkenstein, ed. Karl Kurt Klein. Tübingen 1962 (*Altdeutsche Textbibliothek,* 55).

2. Modern German Translations:

Oswald von Wolkenstein, der mit dem einen Auge, tr. Wieland Schmied. Graz and Vienna 1960 (*Stiasny-Bücherei,* 70). A small selection of Oswald's poetry.

Biographische Gedichte des Herrn Oswald von Wolkenstein, tr. Wieland Schmied. St. Gall, 1963. Small selection.

Oswald von Wolkenstein: eine Auswahl aus seinen Liedern, tr. Burghart Wachinger. Ebenhausen, 1964.

um dieser welten lust: Leid- und Lebenslieder des Oswald von Wolkenstein, tr. Hubert Witt. Berlin: Herbig, 1968. A large selection.

3. Long-playing Record:

Oswald von Wolkenstein. Elf Lieder. Langspielplatte 33 (13042 HP) der Archiv-Produktion des Musikalischen Studios der Deutschen Grammophongesellschaft. (Hamburg, 1956).

4. Linguistic Aids:

SCHATZ, JOSEF, *Sprache und Wortschatz der Gedichte Oswalds von Wolkenstein.* Vienna and Leipzig, 1930 (*Akademie der Wissenschaften in Wien, Phil. -hist. Klasse,* Denkschriften, 69).

TOWNSLEY, LOUIS F. "Glossary to the Songs of Oswald von Wolkenstein." Unpublished dissertation, University of Maryland, 1972.

SECONDARY SOURCES

BANTA, FRANK G. "Dimensions and Reflections: An Analysis of Oswald von Wolkenstein's *Frölich, zärtlich,*" *Journal of English and Germanic Philology,* LXVI (1967), 59–75.

ENGLEMANN, ALFRED. *Oswald von Wolkenstein,* unpublished dissertation, University of Munich, 1951.

FRENZEL, PETER M. "The Episode in the Songs of Oswald von Wolkenstein." Unpublished dissertation, University of Michigan, 1968 (University Microfilms 69–2318).

JACKSON, WM. T. H. "Alliteration and Sound Repetition in the Lyrics of Oswald von Wolkenstein," in: *Formal Aspects of Medieval German Poetry: A Symposium.* Austin: University of Texas Press, 1968, pp. 47–78.

JONES, GEORGE F. "Oswald von Wolkenstein's *Mein sünd und schuld* and the *Beichtlied* Tradition," *Modern Language Notes* LXXXV (1970), 635–51.

LESTER, CONRAD. *Zur literarischen Bedeutung Oswalds von Wolkenstein.* Vienna, 1946 (UCLA dissertation, 1947).

LÖWENSTEIN, HERBERT. *Wort und Ton bei Oswald von Wolkenstein,* Königsberg, 1932 (*Königsberger deutsche Forschungen,* 11).

MANN, OTTO. "Oswald von Wolksteins Natur- und Heimatdichtung." *Zeitschrift für deutsche Philologie* LVII (1932), 243–61.

MARTINI, FRITZ. "Dichtung und Wirklichkeit bei Oswald von Wolkenstein," *Euphorion* XXXIX (1938), 390–411.

MAYR, NORBERT. *Die Reisebilder und Reisen Oswalds von Wolkenstein.* Innsbruck, 1961 (*Schlern-Schriften,* 215).

MÜLLER, ULRICH. *"Dichtung" und "Wahrheit" in den Liedern Oswalds von Wolkenstein.* Göppingen, 1968 (*Göppinger Arbeiten zur Germanistik,* 1).

———. " 'Lügende Dichter?' (Ovid, Jaufre Rudel, Oswald von Wolkenstein)," in *Festschrift für Fritz Martini,* ed. Helmut Kreuzer. Stuttgart, 1968, pp. 32–50.

PETZSCH, CHRISTOPH. "Text- und Melodietypenveränderung bei Oswald von Wolkenstein," *Deutsche Vierteljahrsschrift für Literaturwissenschaft und Geistesgeschichte,* XXXVIII (1964), 491–512.

———. "Die Bergwaldpastourelle Oswalds von Wolkenstein," in: *Sonderheft der Zeitschrift für deutsche Philologie* LXXXVII (1968), 195–222.

SALMEN, WALTER. "Werdegang und Lebensfülle des Oswald von Wolkenstein," *Musica Disciplina,* VII (1953), 147–73.

WENDLER, JOSEF. *Studien zur Melodiebildung bei Oswald von Wolkenstein.* Tutzing, 1963.

Index of Songs Quoted in Text

a. Alphabetical Listing

b. Numerical Listing

107. Kom, liebster
109a. Ave mater
109b. Ave, muotter
110. Ich hör
111. In oberland
112. Mich fragt
113. Ir bäbst
114. Hört zuo
115. Wer hie
116. Zergangen ist
117. Und swig ich
118. Wol auf und wacht
120. Freu dich, du weltlich
122. Wol auf, gesellen
123. Der seines laids
126. Freu dich, durchleuchtig

General Index